ADVANCE PRAISE FOR
THE END OF JOBS

"In the age of the social enterprise, the power of the individual at work is rising exponentially. *The End of Jobs* captures the spirit of this important shift and helps organizations start to think about how worker relationships need to evolve for the future. An important read for any organization trying to compete in the future of work."

—ERICA VOLINI, Global Human Capital Leader at Deloitte

"*The End of Jobs* delves insightfully into the rise of the on-demand economy—and what all of us should expect next. An important read for anyone concerned with automation and the future of work."

—KATHRYN MINSHEW, Founder and CEO, The Muse,
Bestselling Author

"Jeffrey Wald develops a vision of what the workforce of the future will look like as we grapple with convergence, artificial intelligence, and robotics—real factors rapidly shaping the future of work—and real elements being discussed in the executive committees and boardrooms of all companies today. Jeff offers insights that will enable leaders to frame their people strategies as we rapidly scale into an era of the on-demand worker and agile workforce shaped by unimaginable leaps in artificial intelligence applications and robotics."

—DOUG PETERSON, President and CEO, S&P Global

"In this book, Jeff and twenty visionaries paint a detailed picture of the forces shaping the future of work—automation, globalization, remote & freelance work, technology platforms—and how we can ensure a good outcome for all. This book is a must-read for policy makers, business leaders, and anyone interested in the history of work and what it teaches us about possible futures."

—Stephane Kasriel, Former CEO of Upwork,
the world's largest labor marketplace

"Only the creative mind of Jeff Wald could synthesize and articulate this thought-provoking portrait of the future of work! For all organizations, the scope, boundaries, and definition of the global workforce continue to shift and expand, requiring new strategies and management approaches. *The End of Jobs* serves as an integrated guide to thinking through these issues which are undoubtedly on the agenda of leadership teams everywhere."

—Liz Dente, Chief People Officer, Priceline

"As executives think about the future of work, there is no better guide than Jeff Wald's *The End of Jobs*. Jeff's research provides insights into how the future may unfold. Jeff identifies the next wave of technological change as the First Services Revolution, a conclusion that all will come to share. By sponsoring the Future of Work Prize, Jeff has gathered some of the leading labor thinkers, and reading their takes on the world in 2040 was informative and fun!"

—Sreeni Kutam, Chief Human Resources Officer of ADP

"Jeff's outlook on the future of workforce erases the words 'employee,' "contractor," "part-timer," "temp," etc. and suggests a replacement sooner than later with words aligned to the actual work and skills. This is a must for companies and HR leaders to keep pace with this transformation. We must move from jobs and gigs to a new world, perhaps a jig, a skig? Jeff's vision of Total Talent Management is spot on. A company's EVP must be re-engineered in every aspect (the organization, people, work, opportunities, and total rewards). The winners will be the ones that balance the changes brought by mechanization, electrification, and computerization with human experiences that emotionally connect and engage at the individual and team levels."

—Lesley Elwell, Chief People Officer, JE Dunn

"*The End of Jobs* is both a history lesson and a roadmap for the future of labor. The only time I put it down was when I was stopping to contemplate how the book's insights would affect the business that I am in given that we have a large-scale distributed workforce."

—Scott Salmirs, CEO, ABM Industries

"Jeff Wald has written a timely book anticipating that the huge shifts in technology will spark a national focus on building security for America's workers."

—Sara Horowitz, CEO, Trupo, Founder, The Freelancers Union, and Bestselling Author of *The Freelancer's Bible*

"Jeff is widely known as THE expert on our evolving workplace dynamics. His ability to simplify the complex and apply his insights into culture and business is what sets him apart."

—Matt Britton, CEO of Suzy, and Author of *YouthNation*

"In *The End of Jobs: The Rise of On-Demand Workers and Agile Corporations*, author, entrepreneur, and workforce expert Jeff Wald provides an insightful and thoughtful view to the Future of Work. Certainly AI deserves top billing as we consider what the workforce will look like in 2040 but Jeff goes much deeper, highlighting the salient factors contributing to how we arrived where we are as well as where we will be in twenty years—and why. *The End of Jobs* is a compelling read with the added bonus of giving the reader further predictions by some of the industry's most knowledgeable workforce experts."

—Doug Leeby, CEO, IQN/Beeline

"*The End of Jobs* is a must-read for corporate executives who are serious about winning in the next age of talent. Written by a true practitioner in the space, this book takes the reader through a thoughtful and well-structured tour of the reasons for, and implications of, a trend that will profoundly impact how global companies execute."

—Rob Biederman, Co-Founder and CEO of Catalant Technologies

"*The End of Jobs* is a well-written and powerful guide to the future of work. Loaded with facts, statistics, and insights, it is clear-eyed and objective about how companies (and employees) must change to survive."

—MARC EFFRON, CEO, Talent Strategy Group, Bestselling Author of *One Page Talent Management* and *8 Steps to High Performance*

"Supported by over a decade of vast research, Jeff Wald and top thought leaders give extensive insight into the future of work and offer realistic predictions for the future. It will help managers understand how to navigate managing amid sweeping technological and cultural changes, such as retiring workers with all the know-how, millennials desire for work-life balance, and the impact of AI displacing traditional jobs. A must-read for corporate managers or anyone who wants to succeed in the evolving workforce."

—JIM CHOU, Chief Technology Officer, Splice

"A must-read for everyone in the workforce solutions space. Jeff Wald takes his readers into a disruptive near-term future that transforms how companies engage with talent and how society thinks about jobs. The challenge to the talent management industry is clear: we must step up and help guide companies through the next five to fifteen years, or find our own industry rendered obsolete."

—TERESA CARROLL, Former President, Kelly Services

"*The End of Jobs* is a great read for anyone interested in the past, present, and future of work. Jeff Wald, who is and has been an influential leader in the Future of Work era the past decade, shares great insights for those that care about the future of people's economic opportunity."

—EDDIE LOU, Executive Chairman and Co-Founder, Shiftgig

"Artificial Intelligence has more power and influence over the global workforce today than ever before, especially for companies that manufacture and sell products. As CEO of Thinx Inc., I know that society's burgeoning emphasis on AI will impact companies like mine at an unprecedented rate for years to come. In *The End of Jobs: The Rise of On-Demand Workers and Agile Corporations*, Jeff Wald tackles these issues, namely the role that corporations will play in developing AI and how it will impact the future of the global workforce, head on. In the book, Jeff notes the importance of including workers in discussions about corporations integrating AI, and I couldn't agree more. Going forward, I plan to incorporate a more diverse group of voices in our conversations about AI's role at Thinx, Inc. as we continue to grow and evolve. This is a must-read book for business leaders."

—MARIA MOLLAND, CEO of Thinx, Inc.

"This is the best book ever written on any subject."

—PHYLLIS WALD, Jeff's Mom

"*The End of Jobs* is truly a unicorn in the world of business books. If you want to know what to expect in the workplace in 2040, this is your book! *The End of Jobs* provides you with a roadmap for how to work alongside robots and artificial intelligence, and what to expect if your manager is an algorithm!"

—JEANNE C. MEISTER, Founding Partner of Future Workplace, Co-author of *The Future Workplace Experience: 10 Rules for Mastering Disruption in Recruiting and Engaging Employees*

"Insightful and forward-leaning, Wald's book *The End of Jobs* is intentionally provocative. Weaving together his knowledge of the history of work, current workplace norms, early signals, and outlier trends, he provides an optimistic perspective on the rise of the on-demand worker and considerations for the future workplace. Leveraging thought leaders with divergent viewpoints, he offers the reader multiple forecasts on the future of work to stimulate dialogue and predict the future. The variety of perspectives and the weaving together of seemingly unrelated trends creates a must-read (for HR leaders)!"

—CINDY LUBITZ, VP, People Solutions Operations, Cox Automotive

"The nature of jobs is changing faster than any time in history. As founder of WorkMarket, Jeff Wald has been on the front lines of this sea change for years and in *The End of Jobs*, he brings his expertise to the masses in a deeply contextual and digestible way. This book is a must-read for both employees, who need to prepare for the growing dominance of on-demand work, and business leaders, who need to understand how to most effectively structure their talent organizations to remain competitive in this constantly changing world."

—JESSICA MUSE, Former Chief Operating Officer,
Well+Good

"Wald provides an analytical history of the transformation of the American workplace. It should be required reading for MBA students and labor organizers alike."

—BEN GEYERHAHN, CEO, Workers Benefit Fund

"In a constantly evolving service industry founded on creativity where the ideas our workers develop are the product we sell, the insight provided in this book will guide you down the path of striking a new bargain between society and our workers. An approach with Total Talent Management at its core will prepare those of us who run business requiring human interaction and creativity as we face the rise of the Fourth Great Step. There is so much to take from this book—I highly recommend it as you prepare to face the challenges already upon us."

—DEBRA SERCY, Chief Talent Officer, Johannes Leonardo

"I've been lucky enough to know Jeff personally for nearly two decades and the most stimulating discussions I've had around workforce trends have been with him. As an HR professional, I can say Jeff's insight and experience with this topic are unmatched and it was only a matter of time before the world would get to benefit from his unique intellect and perspective. He is truly a pioneer in this space!"

—REBECCA SACHS, SVP, People and Head of
Talent Management at Condé Nast

ALSO BY JEFF WALD

*The Birthday Rules: Critical Conversations
to Have with Your Children (Ages 6–16)*

THE END OF JOBS

THE RISE OF ON-DEMAND WORKERS AND AGILE CORPORATIONS

JEFF WALD

Post Hill
PRESS

A POST HILL PRESS BOOK
ISBN: 978-1-64293-435-9
ISBN (eBook): 978-1-64293-436-6

The End of Jobs:
The Rise of On-Demand Workers and Agile Corporations
© 2020 by Jeff Wald
All Rights Reserved

Interior design and layout by Sarah Heneghan, sarah-heneghan.com.

Post Hill Press
New York • Nashville
posthillpress.com

Published in the United States of America

TABLE OF CONTENTS

INTRODUCTION

ANY STUDY ON THE FUTURE OF WORK (OR THE FUTURE OF ANYTHING) is a "forever" work. The future never comes, it always stretches into the distance—an elusive frontier. So, we continue our study and we make our predictions. We study the past and analyze the present to see what lessons we can learn on how the future may take shape. Because the future of work holds so much influence on how companies, workers, and society function, we are well served to constantly think about how that future may unfold. One thing we do know is that the future of work will bring change, as it always does. While workers may be able to adapt quickly, companies rarely do, and society almost never does. We must try to provide enough insight to those decision makers in government, companies, and households so they can best plan.

Workers need to plan for an unknown future where jobs and benefits are more fluid. Companies need to attract the best talent and remain competitive. Society needs to plan on how best to educate the workforce of the future and provide for those left behind by change.

As the founder of WorkMarket, arguably one of the most transformative pieces of labor software in a generation, I have spent the last ten years researching the history of work and analyzing the current state of the labor markets. I started WorkMarket to help enable companies to efficiently and compliantly organize, manage, and pay their freelancers. We built the software that allowed direct connection between buyers and sellers of labor. We powered billions of dollars of work over millions of tasks for thousands of companies and nearly a million workers.

When I started WorkMarket, the freelance market was predicted to explode. Uber and Lyft were just starting, and everyone thought all companies were moving to an Uber-like on-demand labor model. The prediction that 50 percent of the workforce would be on-demand was commonplace. The largest consulting firms predicted that with the right systems and processes, the $1 trillion in on-demand spending would grow to $3–$4 trillion. Companies needed software to power that transition. Workers needed a simple mobile app to manage their increasingly fluid work arrangements. Thus, WorkMarket was born in 2010.

We were fortunate to raise venture capital from the best investors in the world, and we built our team, working with companies large and small in all kinds of industries. For seven and a half years we grew at breakneck speed before we found a great partner to help drive our growth even further in ADP. ADP is the world's largest human resources company. With over eight hundred thousand corporate customers, there are few companies ADP doesn't work with, providing HR software, payroll services, and a host of other HR and compliance solutions. What they didn't have was a platform in the growing on-demand sector. Consequently, they bought WorkMarket in January 2018.

Being a part of one of the largest companies in the world has massive advantages for the continued deployment of the WorkMarket software, and ADP has been an amazing partner in the writing of *The End of Jobs*. The access ADP can provide to those creating the future of work is unparalleled. With ADP's help I have spoken with hundreds of corporate, union, regulatory, and legal experts in researching this book. I have asked the best of them to contribute directly, as they peer into their crystal balls and tell us all what the world of work will look like in 2040.

Delving into an analysis and predictions on the future of work is vital as we stand at the precipice of a great technological step function: robots and artificial intelligence (AI). This is the fourth great leap forward we have seen in the history of work. The first was mechanization, which began with the dawn of the Industrial Revolution. The second was electrification, as power flowed through the machines. The third was computerization, which created a digital world.

With each change, a shift occurred in the fundamental supply-and-demand relationships between the buyers of labor (companies) and the sellers of labor (workers). Each time, more power accumulated to companies. Technology drove productivity increases that required fewer workers, altering the supply-and-demand balance. We will examine how workers, companies, and society were impacted by these changes in technology and how all three had to come together and renegotiate the social contract. Power imbalances that allowed too much wealth concentration were unsustainable. Other factors in society, like regulation, unions, and the social safety net, had to rise as counterbalancing forces. Balance, or at least stability, emerged each time, along with massive increases to standards of living.

We also see throughout history times when the supply-and-demand balance favors workers. At times when workers have rare skills that allow them to exert power in the relationship, those workers often opt to work in an on-demand capacity. This on-demand aspect of the labor force is an important harbinger for the future of work but not in a way many people believe. We will explore the on-demand labor market, as I believe on-demand labor represents the future state of *all* workers.

This is the focus of our study. How on-demand labor and the three step functions in technological change influenced today's world of work, and what we can learn from the past and present to predict the future of work.

Before we begin, let me first explain our title, *The End of Jobs: The Rise of On-Demand Workers and Agile Corporations*. The "end of jobs" certainly does not mean the end of work, but rather the end of jobs as we have to come to know them; the "in-the-office, one-manager, nine-to-five" job. When I talk about the rise of on-demand workers, that is not to predict that all workers will be Uber drivers. Rather, that the pressures faced by workers in the on-demand market (task-based work, data-driven HR, allocation of tasks by algorithms, and total personal reasonability for your human capital) will increasingly apply to all workers. The "agile corporation" does not mean a company with no full-time employees, but rather the incremental flexibility in employment models (engaging more on-demand labor) that is increasingly required in a rapidly changing world.

While new technologies and the fourth step function of technological innovation will drive change, I will argue in this book that changes to companies' labor models over the near-term will not be nearly as transformative as some predict. However, the change for workers, both on-demand workers and full-time workers, will be profound. Of course, profound change is nothing new for workers.

In *The End of Jobs*, we will examine the abuses workers suffered through the Industrial Revolution and how those injustices led to unions, regulation, and the social safety net. These factors combined to bring about a notion of a Lifetime Employment Contract in post-war America, which brought relative labor peace for companies, workers, and society.

That peace was broken forty years ago. We analyze the confluence of factors that brought the end of the Lifetime Employment Contract and a new reality of work. These factors include shareholder capitalism, globalization, and computerization. Now the worker of today faces new challenges in the post-lifetime-employment world. The world of work has changed from the in-the-office, one-manager, nine-to-five model, to a fluid, team-based, from-anywhere, always-on model. This new world of work was shaped by increased personal responsibility, remote work, and the rise of on-demand labor.

As we move our study toward the future, we look first at what the on-demand labor market can teach us about work's coming evolution. We see how the tensions of the on-demand workers are permeating the full-time labor market. We see how all workers need to prepare for the lack of permanence the on-demand workers live with every day.

The model of exploring the past and analyzing the present leads to my near-term conclusions on the future of work. These are the aspects of work I have a high degree of conviction in predicting. The near-term future of work will include a convergence of on-demand and full-time labor (the rise of on-demand workers) and Total Talent Management (the rise of agile corporations). With convergence, we see all workers own their entire professional life, which some will embrace, and others lament. With Total Talent Management (TTM), companies will become ever more focused on cost with some using the data to treat workers like assets (and invest intelligently) and others using the marketplace to bid work to the lowest cost. These changes of Convergence and TTM are in themselves neither inherently good nor bad for workers. They are trends to be understood and prepared for by workers, companies, and society.

I will then address the looming fourth step function of technological change with robots and AI. The rise of automation and AI has already started and will upend many of today's employment practices. While the first three step functions involved changes to how we make things and were thus the first three industrial revolutions, this change will predominately impact how services are delivered, and thus we will call it the First Services Revolution. Our brief look at this dynamic will contrast the "Skynet" scenario of mankind's doom with the "Rosie Jetson" scenario of technologically driven abundance.

Lastly, we have my favorite part of the book, the Future of Work Prize essays. Here, the twenty greatest leaders in the world of work will offer their visions of the world in 2040. Of the hundreds of interviews I have done for the book, these are the twenty smartest, most influential (and best looking!) leaders, and they agreed to write a few pages on their vision of the future of work. How has the First Services Revolution progressed? How have companies, workers, and society adapted? Each will offer their point of view, unedited for content, and compete for the $10 million Future of Work prize, which I will award on January 1, 2040.

Companies will always need workers, and people will always need incomes. However, in the first two decades of the twenty-first century technological innovation, increasing globalization, and changing demographics have fundamentally disrupted the ways in which these two groups come together for their mutual benefit. The shock waves of that upheaval are rippling out, transforming the concept of jobs and challenging workers, companies, and society to figure out how to respond to the evolving nature of work.

What's the future of work going to look like? I believe we will move closer to an on-demand model for workers, as on-demand workers, and companies, as agile corporations. I believe this will forever change the current notion of "jobs." The only question is how profound and far-reaching these changes will be.

CHAPTER 1

THE HISTORY OF WORK

"Study the past if you would define the future."

—Confucius

TO GAIN INSIGHTS INTO THE FUTURE OF WORK, WE ARE WELL ADVISED to study the past. How can we hope to think about where we are going unless we study where we have been?

> ### What's a job?
>
> 1620s: piece of work; something to be done, contrasted with continuous labor
>
> 1650s: work done for pay
>
> 1722: thieves' slang for theft, robbery, or planned crime
>
> **1858: paid position of employment**

The history of work is a centuries-long story about the shifting balance of power between those that provide work (in recent history, companies) and those that complete work (workers). The vast majority of power has always been with companies. At any point in time, we can study exactly how much of that power companies hold and how much they are willing to use. The power imbalance is almost always due to simple supply and demand. Throughout history, there are usually more workers than there is work. But we will begin our story a bit earlier.

Let's start with this: The word "job" as an employment concept is only about 160 years old. Prior to the first Industrial Revolution there was no real notion of "having a job." People who weren't members of the landed classes, or the clergy, were either peasants working for landlords or artisans with a trade—a skill to market and sell. So, if you were not completely exploited as a peasant, you were an entrepreneur. You studied as an apprentice and developed your skills. You learned how to market those skills to provide for your family. In other words, a freelancer.

What we quickly see, looking at the history of work, is that the on-demand labor model has always existed. Well before the concept of a job was the idea that people provided for their families through a portfolio of work—not by choice, of course, but by necessity. Work was fluid, and a portfolio of activity was necessary to survive.

All that changed when technological advances opened up the possibility of new efficiency gains—and huge profits—to those who could afford to invest in new machinery and build factories. As the first industrial companies began to form around 1800, suddenly there was a need for large-scale, mostly unskilled labor. Lacking a model for this type of interaction, these first employers tended to follow the familiar structure of the landlord-peasant relationship, in which the person who owned the assets held all the power.

The Three Step Functions

Three times before, we have undergone massive change to the relationship between companies and workers. Each time, society ended up better off (more jobs and a higher standard of living) but not before undergoing massive upheavals and, in some cases, a fundamental reordering of the social structure. The breakdowns of these step functions are not clear beginnings and ends, and the implications of the changes wrought by new technology sometimes take decades to materialize. So unfortunately, we are not going to get a nice pattern of: (i) step function happens, (ii) immediately workers are screwed, thus right afterward, (iii) society creates a social safety net.

The lines are just not that clear. What is clear is that for millennia, society had plodded along with minimal economic growth and stable population growth and then the first industrial revolution created a great leap forward on all fronts. Let's now take a very brief (ridiculously brief!) look at the three step functions to ground ourselves in history.

Mechanization

The Industrial Revolution began in England in the mid-1700s and lasted until the mid-1800s. The movement of production from the hands of workers to machines was at the core of this change. During this time, we see the first factories and an explosion of companies, mostly in the textile industry. Innovations like the cotton gin mechanized cotton spinning, and the power loom massively increased productivity and allowed for the mass production of goods.

Let's lay out how certain machines changed the textile industry. A cotton gin could separate cotton from seeds approximately fifty times faster than a human. A mechanized spinner (the spinning jenny or spinning mule were two well-known versions) would spin cotton into usable yarn or thread up to five hundred times faster than a human. Lastly, a power loom could weave that yarn into fabric nearly forty times faster than a human. Each innovation separately was massive but taken together were enough to transform the industry. Britain processed two million pounds of cotton prior to the Industrial Revolution and over six hundred million a few decades later.

Combined with steam power and ironmaking, the Industrial Revolution transformed society. This led to the first significant increases in economic and population growth in human history. Companies were able to use these first machines to engage workers at scale, and they were mostly not kind employers. Workers were pushed to work until they collapsed and were replaced if they complained or couldn't keep up. All the power rested with the companies, and it was a terrible situation for workers. The first regulations were put in place to stop the most egregious abuses, but the first industrial revolution saw the raw impacts of power imbalance. Society advanced with tremendous increases in standards of living. Since this was all so new, and society had never seen such increases in total wealth, the imbalance persisted. There were minimal counterweights to influence the power imbalance. Sadly, it takes decades, sometimes generations, before counterbalancing forces can rise in the world of work.

Electrification

Growth in GDP and populations is then hyper-charged during the second industrial revolution, also called Electrification. This step function began in approximately the late 1800s and lasted to the mid-1900s. Society was again transformed as steam and water power were replaced with electricity in factories in the industrialized world. We see in this era the creation of the communication industry, first with the telegraph and then the tele-phone. The power industry and the electric grid were coupled with steam power on trains and ships to move all industries forward. Steel production and the mass refinement of petroleum helped create the world's first large companies, like US Steel, Standard Oil, and General Electric. With the growth of large corporations, the finance industry rose to support these companies and their needs.

Companies were flourishing, but during this period, we at last see the rise of counterbalancing forces of unions, regulation, and the social safety net. These necessary counterweights allowed for a more stable society and were birthed by many factors, including a period of mass instability and revolutions across Europe in the early-to-mid-1800s. Over the decades it took for these nascent forces to rise, we see tremendous excesses and wealth concentration in the Western world, specifically the United States, as represented in the robber barons. We also see the powerful rising of counterbalancing forces in the US through unions, regulation, and a fun-damental change in the social safety net. The impacts of this period of growth culminated in the Great Depression, and this economic shock allowed for a very rapid renegotiating of the social contract in the US in the New Deal legislation.

This fundamental shift in the structure of society is a regulatory and social safety net response to the imbalances of the first two industrial rev-olutions and set the stage for a period of relative peace in the US often referred to as the Lifetime Employment Model.

Computerization

Beginning in the late 1900s and advancing to today, computerization brings the world its first taste of automation and the creation of an entire new world: a digital universe that creates entire new industries while impacting all existing industries. This third industrial revolution coincides with the industrialization of China, India, and other emerging economies in the birth of globalization. The creation of a global economy, where developing countries get the benefits of the first two industrial revolutions without the necessary counterbalancing forces of regulation, unions, and a social safety net, creates a separate series of imbalances. Workers in these societies face similar abuses to workers in the US and Europe during the first two industrial revolutions.

The impacts of globalization and computerization bring an end to any notion of labor peace in the industrial world. When this is combined with the first robots arriving on the factory floor, we again see companies accumulating power versus workers. This is augmented by the ability to locate production, and then services, to lower-cost countries where the counterweight forces have not developed. This has led to an increasing concentration of wealth for companies and stagnant wages for workers. Society has responded with increased regulation (things like the Occupational Safety and Health Act) and social safety programs (such as the Earned Income Tax Credit). However, the union movement has seen a general decline, and workers, while experiencing an ever-increasing standard of living, are struggling.

Below, we see the impacts of power imbalance in the US, as represented by share of national income (earnings) that goes to the top 10 percent of earners. We see periods of excess lead to radical change and redistribution after the New Deal and the third industrial revolution allowed for more income to flow to the top.

All three step functions bring new industries and new ways of doing work. Each change has huge impacts on society as technology massively increases productivity and companies thus accumulate tremendous power. From corporations to factories, we see the power of companies increase. Then we see the counterbalancing forces of unions, regulation, and the

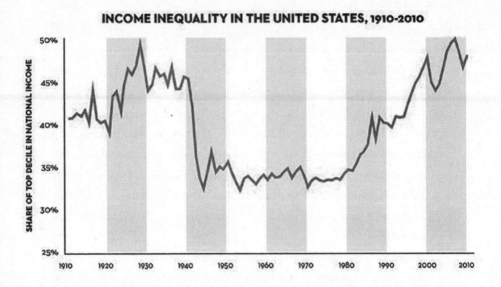

INCOME INEQUALITY IN THE UNITED STATES, 1910-2010

social safety net. Let's expand upon each of these underlying factors in our three step functions.

The Rise of Corporations

The notion of a corporation is thought to date back to the Dutch East India Company, but its history and evolution start much earlier. The idea that a group of people may come together as an entity that conducts business, survives in perpetuity, and has legal rights as a collective was founded in ancient Rome and the Maurya Empire in ancient India.

In medieval Europe, the first corporate entities to spring up seem to be churches. The idea that there existed an entity that persisted beyond the life of a human, and thus that the church's property belonged to the church, was novel. The oldest recorded commercial corporation in the world, the Stora Kopparberg mining community in Falun, Sweden, obtained a charter from King Magnus Eriksson in 1347.

The exploration of the "new world" did lead to the first widely held corporations such as the Dutch East India Company and the Hudson's Bay Company, which were created to lead the colonial ventures of European nations in the seventeenth century. Investors in these companies received paper certificates as proof of share ownership and were able to trade their shares on the first stock exchange in Amsterdam. The company's charter from the king granted limited liability to shareholders in these companies. The corporation as a legal stand-alone entity with limited liability, the hallmarks of the corporate structure, was starting to take shape, but only in concert with royal decree.

However, it is in English common law that we find the most important developments of today's corporations. The first English companies were created by either royal charter or an act of parliament that granted a monopoly over a business or region. The best-known example, established in 1600, was the East India Company of London. Queen Elizabeth I granted it the exclusive trading rights with all countries east of the Cape of Good Hope.

As the Industrial Revolution accelerated, so did the evolution of the laws governing corporations. The Joint Stock Companies Act of 1844 made it possible for citizens to form a corporation without royal decree or act of parliament. However, there was no limited liability in those entities, and company members could still be held responsible for unlimited losses by the company. The next crucial development was the Limited Liability Act of 1855. This allowed investors a limitation on their liability to a failed company; they could now lose only what they invested. This adjustment to corporate law was essential to motivate entrepreneurs who would push the boundaries of industry because it protected them from the threat of unlimited losses.

The last significant development in the birth of the corporate structure was the 1897 British Parliament decision confirming the separate legal personality of the company, with corporate liabilities that were separate and distinct from those of its owners. Corporations now had a legal standing similar to that of individual people.

The solidifying of the limited-liability, stand-alone entity is a crucial part of the world of work. Without these fundamentals, the rest of our history of work would be agonizingly short!

The Rise of Factories

The Venetian Arsenal may provide one of the first examples of a factory in the modern sense of the word. Reportedly founded in 1104 in Venice, it mass-produced ships on "assembly lines" using premade parts.

For thousands of years, work was done by individuals by hand or with crude tools, usually in a field, almost always against their wills. Those individuals might be coordinated by a taskmaster working for the landowner. Mechanisms assisting in performing tasks with limited human interaction were the first force multipliers, and we find examples of machines to farm, capture animals, and grind grain throughout history. But the force multipliers delivered in the field by the use of machinery paled in comparison to what can be achieved with large machines, driven by motors, in factories.

The first factories—where people gathered and took in raw materials, performed tasks, and produced large quantities of finished goods—were founded in England at the beginning of the Industrial Revolution. The factory system was a new way of organizing labor made necessary by the development of machines that were too large to house in a worker's cottage. Working hours were as long as they had been for the farmer—that is, from dawn to dusk, six days per week. One of the earliest known factories was John Lombe's water-powered mill at Derby, founded in 1721. The factory system became more widespread somewhat later when cotton spinning was mechanized.

Richard Arkwright is credited with inventing the prototype of the modern factory. After he patented his water frame (the spinning wheel that harnesses flowing water to turn) in 1769, he established Cromford Mill in England, significantly expanding the village of Cromford to accommodate the migrant workers new to the area (the first company town). Arkwright's factory, and the use of flowing water to generate manufacturing power, showed unequivocally the way ahead for industry and inspired many copies.

Between 1770 and 1850, mechanized factories supplanted traditional artisan shops as the predominant form of producing goods. These larger-scale factories enjoyed a significant technological advantage and lower production costs. The first factories, and indeed the beginning of the first industrial revolution, were centered in England and its textile industry but soon branched out

The Industrial Revolution was advanced further with the force multipliers brought about by the steam engine. Perfected by James Watt in the 1770s, it enabled the rapid development of efficient factories in places where water power was not available. Later generations of steam engines mechanized shoe production and the manufacturing of machinery, including machine tools. Rolling mills, foundries, and locomotive works supported growth in the railroad industry, where steam locomotives greatly expanded the efficiency of railway transportation. The invention of the internal combustion engine took the advances even further and opened new industries to industrialization and an ever-expanding footprint of factories.

Henry Ford further revolutionized the factory concept in the early twentieth century with the innovation of mass production. Highly specialized laborers situated alongside a series of rolling ramps would build up a product such as an automobile. This concept dramatically decreased production costs for virtually all manufactured goods.

In relatively short order—well, about 150 years—we went from the fields to the first factories to engine-powered machinery to production optimization. This great leap forward, driven by mechanization in the way work gets done, had massive implications for the relationship between companies and workers, and for the balance of power between them. Workers went from being abused in the fields to being abused in factories, but with a higher standard of living than ever imagined before.

During the first industrial revolution some factory owners were more concerned with employee well-being than others, but workers had little recourse if they were exploited. Factory work was highly mechanized, so companies didn't need many artisans, just people to manage the machines. Large numbers of workers performed semiskilled or unskilled jobs in assembly lines, turning out virtually identical goods by dividing labor into small task units within uniform processes. Because individuals had become interchangeable cogs in the production line, employers could easily replace workers if they became injured or demanded better treatment or higher wages. Not surprisingly, this power imbalance led to abuse, and that abuse had an equally unsurprising response by workers: rage, action, and unification in a common cause.

The rise of companies and factories during the first industrial revolution and their refinement and the increases in productivity seen in the second and third industrial revolutions meant counterbalancing forces needed to rise. These counterbalancing forces are unions, regulation, and the social safety net. Let's explore their rise.

The Rise of the Unions

As power accumulated to companies due to the rise of factories, workers had to unite to have any hope of maintaining any power in the relationship. The social and economic impacts of the Industrial Revolution led to formation of the first unions in the mid 1800s. The combination of industrialization and urbanization brought workers into closer contact than ever before. With a clear reason (terrible working conditions) and means (they were all together now), organization become a natural next step.

Organized labor started before the Civil War era as local craft unions proliferated in the cities, publishing lists of "prices" for their work and defending their trades against diluted and cheap labor. Central labor bodies first started uniting the craft unions within a single city. The first example of such was the formation in 1827 of the Mechanics' Union of Trade Associations in Philadelphia. In 1852, international unions began organizing local unions of the same craft from across the United States and Canada, starting with the creation of the International Typographical Union. The most powerful were the National Labor Union, launched in 1866, and the Knights of Labor, which reached its peak in the mid-1880s.

Knitting together people living far away into a centralized organizing body proved challenging (a prelude to attempts to unionize on-demand workers today). These large-scale efforts eventually collapsed because of poor organization and strong opposition from employers and government. The American Federation of Labor, founded in 1886, proved a more sustainable model, by uniting various local unions in a loose confederation. The common cause of workers' rights was not enough, so local roots become the focal point of early union successes.

As the companies embraced the factory system and unskilled workers, and used the power imbalance to create horrific working conditions, industrial workers actually were not involved in the early union movement. The craft workers and artisans, perhaps seeing what was happening to workers in factories, and fearing they were next, used the power they still had as highly skilled workers to drive the union movement in the 1800s. Even with all this effort and hundreds of atrocities against the labor movement, only 10 percent of the US labor force belonged to a union by 1920.

New Deal policies in the 1930s drove a surge in union participation. In particular, the National Labor Relations Act (NLRA) of 1935 was a major turning point in American labor history because it put the power of government behind the right of workers to organize unions and bargain collectively with their employers. Driven by the NLRA, post-war America saw collective bargaining become commonplace in the industrial economy, with union membership peaking at 30 percent of the labor force. While union power has clearly waned (membership is back below 10 percent of the labor force), unions were instrumental in achieving for all workers an unprecedented measure of security against old age, illness, unfair working conditions, and unemployment. One of the most important impacts of the union movement was to bring about regulations that could constrain companies and help ease the power imbalance.

There is a fundamental impact that unions have by consolidating the voice of workers into one voice. The power balance is impacted by the company being able to separate workers and thus acerbate the supply and demand imbalance. By bringing workers together in common cause, unions helped bring more power to the workers and thus level the playing field.

The Rise of Regulation

As the factory system allowed for a movement to large-scale production, labor laws become necessary to rein in companies' relative power over workers. With the supply and demand balance massively tilted in companies' favor, workers sought better conditions. In addition, companies wanted regulations in order to have a clear set of rules that all companies had to follow.

As the industrial revolution started in England, England was the first to suffer the consequences of an unregulated power imbalance. Over the course of the late 1700s and early-to-mid-1800s, modern labor law was slowly forming, as some of the more horrifying working conditions were steadily addressed through regulation.

One such issue was the increase in child employment that occurred at the turn of the nineteenth century. As public awareness of children laboring under such egregious conditions increased, the Cotton Mills and Factories Act of 1819 prohibited children under nine years of age from being employed and limited the working day to twelve hours for all workers under sixteen. Another milestone in regulation was reached with the Factory Act of 1833, which restricted (but did not eliminate) the employment of children under the age of eighteen.

In the United States, the majority of labor regulations were codified in the Fair Labor Standards Act (FLSA) of 1938. The FLSA was a wave in the sea change that occurred with FDR's New Deal. The plight of workers deepened so profoundly during the Great Depression that the entire fabric of society was remade through New Deal regulation, which tried to even the playing field between companies and workers. The FLSA required a federal minimum wage and discouraged long hours through time-and-a-half overtime pay. FLSA set the maximum standard work week to forty-four hours, although in 1950 this was reduced further to forty hours. As discussed earlier, the New Deal gave us the NLRA—and, as we will discuss later, the New Deal also played a role in creating the social safety net.

The power of the state was necessary to reign in the labor power imbalance and protect workers.

The Rise of the Social Safety Net

Our third counterbalancing force is the social safety net. With income inequality increasing and power accumulating in the hands of those that provide jobs, the need to further enfranchise workers into the system was heightened. This was answered in the form of the social safety net.

Before we dive into the history of the social safety net, we should set the framework of its three variations. First is a government-sponsored program, the second is employer-sponsored, and the third is individual-sponsored. The government program is focused on the redistribution of wealth in a society—things like welfare, unemployment insurance, and social security are the hallmarks of social safety nets. Employer programs are incentives made to workers for increased productivity and retention that are sometimes required by law. Company programs can include health insurance and retirement plans as well as training and development. Individual safety nets are what we do for ourselves through life insurance, savings accounts, or increasing our own human capital. I will argue later in the book that there is a clear shift toward the individual safety net as governments pull back due to financial constraints and companies pull back due to lower costs.

The government social safety net is a concept of society whereby the state plays a key role in providing for the economic and social well-being of its citizens in order to maintain stability. Many credit legendary German Chancellor Otto von Bismarck with developing the modern social safety net. The measures that Bismarck introduced in 1889 included pensions, accident insurance, and employee health insurance. However, the first Western implementation of a safety net can be found in the Elizabethan Poor Law of 1601. This law cemented the idea that it is the responsibility of the state to provide for the welfare of its citizens, albeit with a distinction between the deserving and undeserving poor, and very limited in scope.

It's vital to note that Bismarck's intention in creating a state-sponsored social safety net was not to deliver fairness, but to bring stability. He talked about the need to prevent an uprising, which would certainly occur if too much accumulated to too few. The intent of the first widespread safety net, and many since, was not to provide for the masses, but to give enough to stop the masses from revolution.

Modern welfare programs are chiefly distinguished from earlier forms of poverty relief by their universal, comprehensive character. The worldwide Great Depression, which brought unemployment and misery to millions, created such an urgent need to help the working class that there was widespread public support for the welfare state in many countries. During the Great Depression, the welfare state was seen as a "middle way" between the extremes of communism on the left and unregulated, laissez-faire capitalism on the right.

> The first Social Security number was issued to John D. Sweeny Jr., age 23: 055-09-0001. He was chosen at random from the first group of people to register on December 1, 1936.
>
> The person with the lowest Social Security number ever issued? Grace Dorothy Owen: 001-01-0001.

The United States was the only industrialized country that went into the Great Depression of the 1930s without national social insurance policies in place. The New Deal changed that. With the Social Security Act of 1935, the United States implemented not only the Social Security program but also the first federal unemployment insurance (done in partnership with the states). New Deal legislation also codified workers' compensation insurance, which had launched in some states in the early 1900s. Social Security and unemployment insurance were followed in 1954 with disability insurance and in 1965 with Medicare and Medicaid.

> The first widespread safety net in the US was the Civil War Pension, which provided payments to former soldiers and their spouses. In 1894, 37 percent of the entire federal budget was spent on these payments. As the program allowed for payments to the surviving spouse (leading to a lot of very old men to marry younger women), the last payment under the program was made in 1999.

Let's take a moment and look at workers' compensation. Workers' comp, as it is known, is an example of a social safety net policy that sought to strike a balance between providing worker protection and giving companies the ability to limit their risk. The basic principles underlying workers' comp are i) that it is mandatory for a company to have, ii) its benefits are provided to the injured worker regardless of who is at fault and, iii) it limits the ability of workers to sue for injuries. This program strikes a balance that has helped keep the peace in labor relations: workers are protected from injury, while companies are protected from lawsuits. Workers' compensation is an excellent example of how regulation can strike the balance between the needs of workers and the needs of companies to the betterment of all.

The Results of Power Imbalance

While corporations were rising, workers were recognizing the need to agitate for their rights. Unions started to form without much success initially, but a generation of violence laid the groundwork for a rebalancing of power. The strong unions, regulations, and the social safety net that resulted continue to influence work even today. All workers owe a debt to the men and women who died over a hundred years ago, and below we spotlight some of the most horrible events and their impacts.

Homestead Strike: Organized, Purposeful, and Stained with Blood

The Homestead Strike was an industrial lockout and strike that took place in Homestead, Pennsylvania, in the first week of July 1892. Labor historians see it as a prelude to modern strikes due to the level of organization among workers.

Negotiations for a new collective bargaining agreement with Carnegie Steel led the company to lock out its workers from the steel mill. Carnegie was planning to reopen the mill with a nonunionized workforce. The strikers ringed the mill and fighting broke out when Carnegie Steel tried to bring in strikebreakers and Pinkerton security agents. Joined by the state militia, the Pinkerton agents violently broke the strike, killing twelve workers.

We see in the Homestead Strike the first large-scale use of the military and private security. The violence and death that resulted caused widespread fear among working-class America. This incident became the first rallying cry and started to galvanize American laborers to take action.

The Pullman Strike: A Strike That Impacted the Nation

The Pullman Strike was a nationwide railroad strike in the United States that lasted for three months in 1894, shutting down much of the nation's freight and passenger rail traffic. It began when the Pullman Company (a manufacturer of rail cars) reduced wages but kept rents at company-owned housing the same, severely impacting the employees living in its company town. Nearly four thousand employees of Pullman began a wildcat strike, and the American Railway Union supported them with a call for a boycott against trains with a Pullman car (virtually every train). Violence broke out, the army was called in, and the strike collapsed with nearly thirty people dead.

The Pullman Strike was a major turning point in the public consciousness of the labor movement. As it impacted the railways, the arteries of the nation's economy, it is the first time the entire country paid close attention to a labor strike.

The Ludlow Massacre: The First Action That Led to Legislation

The Ludlow Massacre was one of the deadliest single incidents of labor conflict in the US. The massacre occurred during a prolonged strike by mine workers in Colorado starting in 1914.

The main incident occurred on April 20, 1914, at Ludlow, Colorado. The Colorado National Guard and Colorado Fuel and Iron Company guards attacked a tent colony of 1,200 striking coal miners and their families, firing machine guns into the colony. About two dozen people, including miners' wives and children, were killed. Following the massacre at Ludlow, miners armed themselves and attacked dozens of anti-union establishments over the next ten days, destroying property and engaging in several skirmishes with the Colorado National Guard. An estimated 199 deaths occurred during the entire strike.

The Ludlow Massacre was a watershed moment in American labor relations. The chief owner of the mine, John D. Rockefeller Jr., was widely condemned for having orchestrated the massacre. Public outrage helped propel passage of the Adamson Act of 1916, which included the first federal eight-hour workday.

Battle of Blair Mountain: Transforms Union Tactics Away from Violence

The Battle of Blair Mountain was the single bloodiest labor insurrection in US history and is recognized as one of the largest, best-organized, and most well-armed uprisings since the American Civil War.

The conflict occurred in West Virginia in 1921 as part of the Coal Wars—a series of early-twentieth-century labor disputes in Appalachia. Tensions rose as miners attempted to unionize the West Virginia coalfields. This led to a standoff with some ten thousand armed coal miners confronting three thousand lawmen and the West Virginia National Guard.

From late August to early September violence raged. By the time the US Army arrived to end the strife, nearly two hundred were dead. The coal mine operators—with the support of law enforcement and the military—triumphed, and the United Mine Workers saw membership plummet from more than fifty thousand miners to approximately ten thousand over the next several years.

The Battle of Blair Mountain was the last major armed conflict of the US Labor Movement. The loss of life, the breaking of the strike, and the decline in union membership showed union leaders that new tactics were needed. Union focus shifted to political and public relations battles.

Triangle Shirtwaist Factory Fire: Leads to Better Workplace Safety Standards

The Triangle Shirtwaist Factory fire in New York City on March 25, 1911, was one of the deadliest industrial disasters in US history. During the fire, 146 garment workers (mostly women) died, suffering from smoke inhalation and falling or jumping to their deaths. The owners had locked the doors to the stairwells and exits, a common practice to stop workers from taking breaks and stealing.

The fire led to legislation requiring factory safety standards and helped propel the further growth of the union movement. As the first front-page labor incident, the Triangle Fire became a rallying cry for workers and the general population.

The Jungle: Led to the FDA

The Jungle, a book written in 1906 by Upton Sinclair, portrayed the harsh conditions of the meat industry and the exploited lives of immigrants in Chicago and similar industrialized cities in the early twentieth century. It focused on working-class poverty, appalling factory conditions, and the pervasive hopelessness among many workers. It also exposed the unsanitary practices in the meatpacking industry during the early twentieth century.

After reading the book, President Theodore Roosevelt ordered an investigation with a formal report to Congress in June 1906. Public pressure led to the passage of the Federal Meat Inspection Act and the Pure Food and Drug Act; the latter established the Bureau of Chemistry (in 1930 renamed as the Food and Drug Administration). This directly led to better working conditions and a more sanitary work environment for all workers.

All the incidents we highlight just scratch the surface of the horrors US workers faced during a period where the power balance strongly favored companies. Many thousands more died due to poor safety standards. Mining alone saw approximately twenty thousand deaths from industrial accidents from 1900–1910. With rising inequality, long-standing abuse of the power imbalance, and poor working conditions leading to deaths in the tens of thousands of workers, something had to rise to bring a balance back.

The Rise of the Lifetime Employment Contract

The rise of companies and factories tilted power to employers. Horrific abuse of that power—as showcased in *The Jungle*, the Triangle Fire, and the destruction wrought by labor disputes—shifted public opinion and helped the rise of unions. Union expansion and increasing public outrage helped drive labor regulations and deploy the social safety net as workers gained some power back from companies.

And then the peace came.

It wasn't a perfect peace, but the balance of power was stable enough, with regulation constraining company power, unions empowering workers, and the social safety net imparting a sense of security. As the wave of technological change abated and the world settled into a post-war Pax

Americana, global stability supported an employment truce in which companies and workers engaged in an unwritten Lifetime Employment Contract (LEC). Companies would employ people for life, take care of training and development, and provide for retirement and healthcare. In exchange, people would work and dedicate themselves to a given company as they marched toward the "gold watch."

In this model, unions helped ensure mass employment of their members, winning clearly defined benefits and opportunities to advance and build careers. Employers benefited from the labor stability that unions could provide and came to see human resources as assets. In that context, talent retention and training were wise investments in the development of the company. For many people, hiring was the beginning of a predictable progression through layers of the company hierarchy, with a well-funded retirement soon after. Though there was still unfairness in the labor market, alongside occasional strikes and unrest, this social contract served all parties involved.

We will address later what the data tell us about how widespread a concept the Lifetime Employment Contract was. Regardless of how many workers had access to the Lifetime Employment Contract, it was the prevailing aspiration of the workforce and an important notion of work. Until it wasn't.

CHAPTER 2

THE BREAKING OF THE LIFETIME EMPLOYMENT CONTRACT

"Only satisfied customers can give people job security.
Not companies."

—Jack Welch

THE LIFETIME EMPLOYMENT CONTRACT (LEC) HAS BEEN BROKEN. EVEN as a tacit expectation of partnership, a model for lifetime employment seems to have gone extinct. What is interesting is the romanticized notion of the LEC despite how short (and not widespread) this period was. The period of LEC was an aberration in the history of work, a rare peace between the buyer and the seller. While the LEC was more aspirational than factual, it still echoes through conversations about labor today.

The LEC was more a function of less competition than some stated truce. The LEC came to be after the New Deal and the end of World War II. During this period, US companies were insulated from much global competition as Europe was rebuilding and the emerging economies of the world had not yet arisen. In a world with little competitive threat, making lifetime promises and granting ever-growing wage increases were good for business. But it couldn't, and didn't, last.

There are several interdependent forces that conspired to break the LEC: shareholder capitalism, globalization, and computerization. We will delve into each, examining how they intersect and what roles they played in eroding the glue that bound workers and companies together.

Shareholder Capitalism

As the corporate model evolved, so did the philosophies on whom corporations serve. Various approaches have dominated financial thinking over the years. Companies exist to serve the public good. Companies exist to serve the communities in which they operate. Companies exist to serve all their stakeholders, including their employees.

One point of view that came to prominence in the 1970s was that companies exist solely to serve the interests of their shareholders. We call this shareholder capitalism. While this notion seems commonplace today, it was not always the sole point of view of company boards and executives. One of the main differences in approach to management under shareholder capitalism is that workers start to be viewed as a cost to be managed and not as talent to be nurtured.

> The CFO says to the CEO, "What if we train all our workers and then they leave?"
> The CEO responds, "What if we don't and they stay?"

When companies pursue a narrow definition of shareholder value, as defined by increasing the value for shareholders, it may no longer makes sense for them to invest in training and developing employees. The less employers commit to employees' long-term careers, the less employees commit to the company.

With companies focused on shareholder value, managers look to be as responsive to market forces as possible. The more responsive a company could be at adjusting its costs to revenue, the greater return it could deliver to shareholders. But it's virtually impossible to run an agile corporation when managers have limited flexibility on their largest cost: labor. Companies found that having a fixed labor force put them at a competitive disadvantage because they couldn't change their workforce quickly in response to changing market conditions.

Incentive structures of management reflected this new focus on short-term targets. This short-term thinking became a hallmark of shareholder capitalism and of management incentive plans. As companies grow in size and scope, and compensation is tied to profit margins, managers tend to reduce staff (especially faraway staff they will never meet) in order to meet short-term goals and get paid their bonuses.

At the same time, a problem was developing with another aspect of the lifetime employment model: defined-benefit pension plans were running into trouble. For decades, companies had committed to paying certain guaranteed amounts to retired workers for the rest of their lives. This was the core of the employer social safety net. But now, with people living longer after retirement, the costs of those retirement plans shot up, becoming much higher than anyone ever anticipated. And those companies offering retirees medical coverage faced dramatically rising costs due to increased healthcare expenses and longer lifespans. The true costs of the lifetime employment model began to hit businesses hard.

One of the first formal company pensions was introduced in 1882 by a builder of pianos, the Alfred Dodge Company. Dodge withheld 1 percent of his workers' pay for a pension and the company added to the fund. Sadly, the company went out of business a few years later, making the Dodge Pension Plan one of the first to fail.

By 1900 there were only five companies in the US offering pension plans, and as late as 1932, only 15 percent of workers were in a pension plan.

A General Electric HR executive succinctly expressed the dominant sentiment of the 1980s when he exhorted employees to "do good work, work hard, and always have a copy of your résumé ready" because "as a society, we're going to be moving away from the things that tie people to a company for thirty years."

With companies and managers focused acutely on the bottom line, and the costs of the lifetime employment model rising (or becoming apparent), companies started to dissolve the glue that held together the LEC.

Globalization

Another source of pressure on companies and the LEC was globalization. While the increasingly interconnected global economy means more markets for companies to sell their goods and services in, it also means a global labor market. As we think about the power balance that exists between workers and companies, I am not sure of any factor that so brutally impacted workers' power in that relationship than globalization. While there are innumerable benefits to globalization, the basic laws of supply and demand put a massive amount of power back to companies as, rather suddenly, there was a huge influx of new workers in a newly global labor market.

Back in the postwar period, when the LEC was taking shape, companies were somewhat buffered from global competition. There wasn't much manufacturing in emerging markets, for example, and even the highly developed European countries were struggling to get back on their feet after the tremendous damage to their infrastructure sustained during the war.

As the Chinese, Indian, and other emerging economies started to industrialize in the 1980s, new companies with much lower costs of production began to compete in global markets. In so doing, they were essentially unleashing nearly a billion workers from an agrarian economic model into the global industrial workforce. Many of these people were cheap to employ; they lived in countries with much lower costs of living and limited expectations of lifetime employment or benefits. It must be noted that companies, both foreign and domestic, operating in these countries did not face the same regulatory, social, and union structures that workers in the US and EU had fought for and won. The sweatshops moved from the Triangle factories of New York to the mass production lines of China.

Through the laws of supply and demand, this huge influx of new workers led to widespread stagnation of wages in the West over the past forty years. We can argue many points, but the basic laws of supply and demand are tough to escape—and supply just increased massively.

Companies in the US with a large base of full-time employees suddenly found they were competing against companies with a much lower cost model. Companies that shifted operations overseas paid less for hourly wages and less (or even nothing) for health benefits or pensions.

This new workforce led to tremendous cost-saving opportunities. Those cost savings allowed managers to not only please their shareholders but also stay competitive with a new breed of companies competing against them in the global market.

As an example of differing regulations and their impacts on workers, we can look at coal mining safety in the US with information from the US Energy Information Administration. Throughout the 1900s, until just after the New Deal, deaths of coal miners in the US measured in the thousands annually (reaching a terrible peak of 3,242 in 1908). Through the influence of unions and regulations, annual deaths in coal mining dropped to the hundreds through 1970, then to the double digits with a record low of 8 deaths in 2016 (for a 0.01 percent rate). Of course, this is not just the result of safer mines, but also fewer coal workers, as automation drove employment in coal from nearly 800,000 in the 1900s to 200,000 in 1960 and about 80,000 today. Another important factor in the study of coal is productivity, with a miner in the 1900s producing about 337 short tons of coal annually (total production in the US in 1900 was 270 million short tons) compared to a miner today producing approximately 9,437 short tons (total production today is 755 million). So yes, there are fewer coal miners, but total coal produced in the US is much higher.

If we were to compare this to coal production and safety in an emerging economy, we see some interesting comparisons. According to the Chinese Academy of Social Sciences there are 5.2 million coal workers in China today who produce 3.45 billion short tons of coal. Thus, the productivity of a Chinese coal worker is 663 short tons annually, or about double a US worker in 1900, but fourteen times less productive than a US coal worker today. In addition to not being as productive, there are about 2,000 reported deaths from coal accidents in China today for a rate of 0.04 percent, or four times the rate for a US worker today.

In this one quick comparison, we see employment much higher and productivity and safety standards much lower in China. We see how safety and productivity improved over time in the US but with a massive decrease in employment. I have no doubt that productivity improvements will come to Chinese mining, but an improvement in their safety and pay is less assured in the near term, although I believe inevitable in the long term.

Conditions of labor in emerging markets mirror those in the West at the beginning of the twentieth century, meaning terrible at best. The labor markets are still struggling to find equilibrium. Workers in emerging markets are now demanding more protections, higher wages, and an increased say in society. Workers and companies in the West deal with stagnant wages and a post-lifetime employment model. Wherever and whenever equilibrium is reached, one thing is certainly true: this influx of new workers, holding a different set of expectations and rights, tore apart the glue binding companies and workers together.

Computerization

Technological change has always impacted the way we work and always will. From the three step functions of technological change we see technology powering productivity gains, or new industries, that change work patterns. The third industrial revolution was gaining speed just as the LEC was in full force as an idea. Computerization impacted the LEC in three critical ways: it untethered many jobs from a formal workplace, led to a demand for scarce new skill sets that changed the balance of power, and drove the rise of automation that de-skilled or eliminated many jobs.

The rapid development of mobile technologies has greatly reduced the need for a physical workplace. The refinement of video communication has allowed real-time "in-person" meetings to take place between people a world apart. Email, IM, Slack, and other collaboration tools make the physical presence of a person nearly irrelevant. Down the hall, on another floor, down the block, or a thousand miles away—all feel like the same distance in today's world of work.

While many traditional organizations preferred to keep their workers in the office, start-ups quickly embraced mobility and its associated benefits. On-demand workers who often can't be in the same locations were at the forefront of this trend. While some workers are slow to adopt new technologies (we all know the boss who insists on face-to-face meetings), a new generation of workers, accustomed to 24/7 access to smartphones and other digital technologies, is pushing the boundaries of the norms of work. New technologies are creating a new world of work where everyone need not be in the same place in order to be on the same team. The more remote the workforce, the more frayed the LEC.

Another powerful impact of technology on the lifetime employment model is the need for digital skills in the era of computerization. Technology can proliferate so quickly that those who tap into these skill sets boost their demand faster than the education system can produce workers with the right skills. This leads to a temporary but powerful supply and demand imbalance that massively favors those workers. Digital skills—such as e-commerce, digital marketing, and software programming—came into demand so quickly at the turn of the century that the people with these skill sets had the majority of the power in this economic relationship between the buyer and the seller of labor. These people could set their own terms, and increasingly, those terms were, "I will come work with you, but only as a freelancer."

This shift in the power balance meant, for the most part, that these workers were able to make the money they wanted, while working the way they wanted from the places they chose. Even now that the talent shortage in digital skills isn't as acute as it once was, companies have become accustomed to engaging technologists on an on-demand basis.

This time the glue binding the LEC was pulled apart by workers. Those who could set the terms of their employment did so in a way that provided them more freedom to choose where and when they worked. They chose lifestyle over lifetime and forged the way for all workers who wanted to follow.

While entirely new types of job skills were coming into existence, many more were being de-skilled or eliminated. Technology has always created the productivity improvements needed for economic growth, but also can increase productivity to the point that fewer workers are needed. This is true all the way back to our first innovation in the textile industry. Millions of workers in the fields and making textiles at home were replaced with tens of thousands in factories. This is also true during the computerization change that occurred as the LEC broke. Manufacturing saw not only the outsourcing of jobs to lower-cost geographies, but also the first wave of robots on the factory floor. Those robots allowed for much greater output but with the same or fewer workers.

Whether it's coal miners being replaced by machines that rip coal from the ground or assembly line workers being replaced by robots, the trends are unmistakable. In hundreds of different ways, computerization eliminated the need for some workers. Instead of training someone, paying them, and taking care of them in retirement, a company often just needs a machine or a software program—and they can own it and work it until it breaks. It seems the only glue left in this relationship is the glue holding parts of the computer together.

Shareholder capitalism demoted workers to a fixed cost to be minimized. Globalization created a massive and still-adjusting supply-and-demand imbalance. Technology broke the nine-to-five, in-office life, creating skills shortages and automating jobs away. Is it any wonder the LEC crumbled?

Before we examine the new world of working, let's look at some examples of how the breaking of the LEC actually happened at some of the greatest companies of our time.

The End of Lifetime Employment: How It Actually Happened

For a close-up look at how these three factors—shareholder capitalism, globalization, and computerization—conspired to end the LEC, consider two great companies: IBM and Estée Lauder and what is publicly available about their stories of change.

A Near-Death Experience at IBM Due to Globalization and Technology Changes

There is an informal class system at IBM, in which workers were either categorized as Deep Blue or Light Blue. In the 1980s and before if you were

Deep Blue, you'd been hired and spent months being trained in the IBM Way—IBM would virtually never let you go. Some said that "IBM"was an acronym for "I've Been Moved" because of the company's propensity for moving employees rather than firing people trained in the IBM way. Your job would evolve and change, but you'd still be Deep Blue. IBM valued Deep Blue employees' commitment, skills, and training, and Deep Blue employees represented about 90 percent of IBM's workforce. Light Blue employees, however, were just cheap, replaceable contractors with lower statuses than the Deep Blue "permanent" staff.

Entering the 1980s, IBM found itself trying to operate with a large fixed-cost workforce while shouldering the burden of supporting a large and growing retiree population of Deep Blue workers. The company was struggling to compete with the new, more agile technology companies (many from emerging markets) because its workforce couldn't adapt and its payments to retirees reduced the funds available to invest in growth.

The company came very close to bankruptcy as new technology and foreign competition rose, necessitating IBM's first series of mass layoffs. Though it was neither the first nor the last company to break the LEC, IBM's sheer size and public profile meant its decision sent a clear signal to companies and workers everywhere.

The IBM of today would be nearly unrecognizable to an IBMer of the 1980s. While Deep Blue employees still show up every day in the office, they may no longer feel that IBM is making a commitment to providing them a lifetime of professional growth and employment. Meanwhile, they're working alongside an increasing number of Light Blue contractors. Those team members come and go as they please, have more control over what work they take on, have more control over their working hours, and have more bargaining power over their pay. The trade-off, of course, is that Light Blue workers do not get the same benefits and security afforded to their Deep Blue cohorts. However, with those benefits and job security looking less enticing, the Light Blue trade-off looks more and more attractive. Today's IBM is estimated to be 50 percent Deep Blue and 50 percent Light Blue—and Light Blue workers are no longer considered second-class citizens.

The Need for New Skill Sets Brings Change to Estée Lauder

At the turn of the century Estée Lauder had approximately forty thousand full-time employees, very few on-demand workers, and the vast majority of its staff was female. Some would say the main job of Estée employees was protecting and growing the company's stable of brands. A huge amount of value for Estée lies in the power of their famous brands. Those brands are desired all over the world and convey luxury and beauty to consumers. Because of the importance of the brands, Estée did not engage many on-demand workers who, as outsiders, were not trained on how to represent each of those brands.

However, as the world moved rapidly online in the late 1990s, Estée found itself struggling to hire the digital talent that was needed. As the company decided it needed to develop its e-commerce and digital marketing capabilities, it was tasked with onboarding people with these emerging-technology skill sets, quickly and in large numbers. The digitization of Estée Lauder created a huge challenge for two reasons: most people with those digital skill sets didn't want to work full-time, and most of them were men. As we discussed previously, there was a huge supply-and-demand imbalance in favor of workers with digital skills. Those workers were simply not looking for a nine-to-five job at a company like Estée. As for why most of those with digital skills at the time were men, well, that is another subject and book entirely.

In order to quickly become a digital company, Estée had to change, and it did, rapidly. Estée engaged independent contractors en masse and put in place processes to ensure brand identity was protected. Estée Lauder reportedly now has approximately fifteen thousand on-demand workers, and their culture and processes have evolved to allow them to hire the best people, however those people want to work.

The changes at these great companies were harbingers for companies and workers in all industries. Rapid change and fierce low-cost competition were the new norm. Companies had to become more agile. Workers had to prepare for less company safety nets and prepare to take more responsibility for their health care, retirement, training, and development.

CHAPTER 3

WHERE ARE WE NOW?

"The future depends on what you do today."

—Gandhi

OUR GOAL IS TO LOOK AT THE PAST AND ANALYZE THE PRESENT SO that we can make meaningful predictions about the future of work. So where is the world of work now? Where is the power balance that defines the world of work? How have workers and companies adapted in a post-lifetime-employment world? What are the biggest factors impacting companies and workers today?

In studying the labor force trends of today, we can see what dynamics have survived the breaking of the LEC and step function changes in technology. Those trends that have persisted through the history of work may provide a strong indication of the future of work.

While the LEC may have been more myth than fact, when shareholder capitalism, globalization, and technology killed the LEC, they did change the world of work. Work was structured in an in-the-office, one-manager, and nine-to-five model. The end of the notion of the LEC started the end of this model and brought us to a more fluid world of work. This doesn't mean people change jobs more frequently (they don't); it means that the nature of their jobs is changing rapidly.

The old model meant reporting to a manager, who would dole out assignments. While people still have managers, as work continues to get atomized into projects and tasks, those projects and tasks have to be done in coordination with other teams. This task-based work has created lots of interdependence. Tasks that were broken up need to be put back together as an end product. Think about a marketing plan being broken into several tasks with individuals working on parts like social media, lead generation, brand, and so on, and someone bringing all the parts together for the final delivery of a full marketing plan. This means work is interdependent, requiring coordination across teams and departments and with outside experts.

Tasks necessitate a fluid, team-based approach to work. Teams form, projects are tackled, and the team disbands. Most workers are staffed on several cross-functional teams and have a matrix of reporting structures. They still have their "review" with their direct boss on the "org chart" but that person spends less and less time directly working with their "org chart" teams. This is one of the reasons why the annual review is giving way to more frequent check-ins with teams; bosses need to know what their people are actually working on. Combine this with the fact that our devices and communication software mean we are always tethered to our jobs (even if we haven't been to our actual desk in weeks) and we are always on the job. Remote work has also become a standard in today's world of work, but more on that later.

As the org chart gives way to a fluid, team-based approach to work, the large enterprise software firms are catching up. ADP's next generation of HR software allows visibility into, and management of, the teams. The ADP software lets a manager track each team member's progress and projects. Regardless if your team includes outside vendors, freelancers, temps, colleagues from across the globe, and even your own boss, software now allows the management of the actual work team members are doing.

This is the new model of work: fluid, team-based, from anywhere, and always on.

This new labor model is defined by a series of forces that echo not only the history of power imbalance tilted toward companies, but also the changing face of society. Whether it's technology or demographic shifts, the factors influencing our lives tend also to influence our work. We will explore these factors to better understand which are most likely to influence the future of labor (we will explore the hard data in the next chapter). The most important trends of today's labor market are:

- ▶ On-demand labor
- ▶ Remote work
- ▶ Income inequality
- ▶ Increased personal responsibility

On-Demand Labor

While the refrains of "everyone's going to be an Uber driver in the future" and "all jobs created in the last ten years are on-demand jobs" are simply not borne out in the labor data, the on-demand economy is approximately 25–30 percent of the labor force (more on this later). While this represents a massive part of labor, it may not be as large, or growing as fast, as some would say.

I will argue that the on-demand economy is approximately the same size as it was thirty years ago but has become more prominent due to some structural changes that have occurred.

It used to be that when a recession hit, companies would let go of some of their full-time staff. As a recovery started to emerge, companies would dip their toes in the water and hire workers as temps and freelancers. When the recovery solidified, companies would convert those temps and freelancers to full-time employees. This left a counter-cyclical on-demand market that would grow during downturns and decrease in upturns. My best estimate from reading every study on on-demand labor and my experience at WorkMarket is the on-demand labor force has counter-cyclically moved between 20 and 30 percent of the labor force over time. However, during the end of the 2007–2008 recession, also called the Great Recession, I believe we have seen some divergence from past countercyclical patterns.

Despite the fact that we have experienced the longest economic expansion in US history, on-demand workers have not, for the most part, converted to full-time employees. I believe there are three reasons for this: technology, the type of recession, and social acceptance.

Vendor Management System (VMS) technology helps companies efficiently and compliantly manage their temp workforces in partnership with their staffing vendors, who find and payroll those temps. Freelance Management System (FMS) technology helps companies directly organize, manage, and pay their freelance workers. One of the biggest gaps in engaging on-demand labor is the efficiency of bringing resources in and out of the company. With VMS and FMS technology, you create not only tremendous efficiency but also help mitigate compliance risk. Now that companies have systems that make it easier and safer for them to engage these workforces, there's less reason to convert them to full-time. This has led to growth in on-demand labor even though only large companies use VMS software and FMS software is still in its infancy.

This was also influenced by the depth of the Great Recession. The Great Recession was deep and debt-driven, and its recovery was slow and shallow. With a slower recovery, we would expect different behaviors from companies than those in a sharp recovery. The slow and shallow nature of the recovery may have impacted the on-demand economy and thus contributed to the decoupling and growth.

The psychographic change is more abstract. For many reasons, people increasingly want to work in an on-demand capacity. They want the flexibility. They want the variety of projects. The example of Deep Blue and Light Blue switching at IBM is important here. Twenty years ago, the term "freelancer" really meant "unemployed." Today it means "entrepreneur." I believe platforms like Uber, Lyft, Handy, and Rover have brought awareness of the on-demand economy into our daily lives, making it a widely accepted and understood part of the modern work market. Workers today commonly refer to their "side hustle" as a normal component of their work life. While the economic necessity of an increasing number of workers to have a side hustle is another issue, the technological and psychographic changes have helped propel the on-demand workforce to the forefront of labor resource planning and to the front page of the paper.

We will touch upon on-demand labor much deeper later in the book. While it is not a new phenomenon in the labor market, it will have a powerful impact on the future of work.

Remote Work

As we discussed previously, remote work is a common feature of today's workforce due to advancements in technology and social choice. The use of video conferencing and collaboration tools have made it possible for anyone to work remotely. Again, tools like Slack, IM, Skype, and many more make collaboration regardless of distance not only possible but also practical—ever more practical as the costs of this type of software have decreased.

Accelerating this trend was the increasing adoption of technologies at home through either the worker's mobile device or home connectivity. Slack isn't that helpful if I can only access it at my desk in the office. But technology alone isn't enough; people have to want to work remotely before they'll adopt these new tools.

Among the first remote workers were those in emerging markets like India (software programmers) and the Philippines (call centers) that connected to companies through on-demand labor platforms. Work that was easily broken into tasks like a quick coding assignment or a logo design were done using pioneers like oDesk, Elance, and Freelancer.com, which emerged at the turn of the century. This allowed for the use of workers across the planet, combining our trends of remote work and global labor markets. With these tools you could watch your remote team member's keystrokes or their actual engagement through a webcam (with their permission).

The social dynamics of working remotely have changed. Gone are the days when working remotely meant social isolation. Now it means being able to focus your time, work efficiently, balance work and life, and stay in touch through collaboration tools.

The emergence of coworking offices like WeWork and Knotel are driven by, and help continue to drive, the remote work trend. Now any company can have a location where remote team members can gather as needed, or work outside of the home in an open office environment, replete with all the adornment of a modern tech office. Home isolation is replaced with a vibrant office setting. Whether because companies allow it, technology enables it, or people choose it, remote work has now become a key part of working today.

Income Inequality

Income inequality in the United States has fluctuated through our working history. While data prior to 1900 is tough to come by, there is a sense that income distribution was rather stable for much of the history of the United States, with only periodic spikes. One such spike corresponded with the beginning of electrification and the robber barons. However, this spike in inequality was wiped out with the Great Depression. Estimates show that the top 1 percent of income earners in the US during that period earned about 20 percent of all income. After the Great Depression and the New Deal, the income of the top 1 percent returned to its historic average of about 10 percent. It broadly stayed at 10 percent through the period of the LEC.

As shareholder capitalism, globalization and technology conspired to break the "in-the-office, one-manager, nine-to-five" job, we again saw income inequality rise. These trends were coupled with a lowering of the top margin tax rate from 91 percent in the 1960s to 70 percent in the 1970s, to 28 percent after the Tax Reform Act of 1986. The top 1 percent of earners started accumulating more of the country's income, rising through the 1980s and 1990s to return to 20 percent of total income in the 2000s. This increase has continued, and the top 1 percent today are earning approximately 25 percent of all income today.

This trend is a powerful force in the current labor market. Income inequality drives debates on minimum wage, immigration policies, unions, and almost every other aspect of the world of work. According to the Economic Policy Institute the average CEO pay is now nearly 300 times that of the average worker. In the 1970s it was roughly 30 times. Clearly, income inequality by most measures has gotten worse.

Arguments can be made as to why this increase has occurred and should be our policy responses. Whatever the reason and whatever we decide to do, it is important to recognize that history shows that this increase in income inequality is not sustainable. Eventually workers will demand or vote for a policy response. This can come in the form of higher taxes on income, capital, or wealth, or in the form of increased social safety net programs. Those two should go hand in hand, as any increase to the government safety net should be coupled with increased revenue to pay for it, but that may be too rational for our politics. What is clear is that income inequality remains an important facet of the world of work today and will have a substantial impact on the future of work if left unchecked.

Increased Personal Responsibility

Not surprising with the breaking of the LEC, companies are taking less responsibility for workers' development and welfare: a pullback of the employer safety net (which included training and professional development). This has led to an inevitable increase in workers' personal responsibility for their skill development and their own welfare. Workers have to step in and take ownership of their retirement plans, their healthcare plans, and their career development. This shift from an employer safety net to an individual safety net has led many to call for an increase in the government safety net.

Clearly, today's workers do not have the same total responsibility for their welfare as their on-demand counterparts, but the trends are pointing in that direction. Gone are the days of weeklong training junkets. It's important to remember that personal responsibility does not just apply to health care, retirement, and insurance. It also applies to training and development. These used to be the purview of companies, but companies are increasingly pushing it down to the workers. One of the most illuminating examples comes from a large technology company where a long-time employee explained:

> Twenty years ago, we used to have weeks of trainings. Trips to get together and learn about the newest tech, to build relationships with our colleagues. There was even a company sponsored university complete with full-time staff. Now we all have to find forty hours of our own time, outside of normal work hours, to complete

mandatory online training. No trips, no university, just our own time on our own dime.

We have seen the virtual disappearance, outside of the public sector, of the pension plan and health care for life. Even in the public sector, with by far the strongest unions, we see workers contributing more to their health care and new employees not being given the same long-term promises. For many reasons, personal responsibility is now a hallmark of the modern work market. The reality of personal responsibility on the future of work is becoming clear.

Each of these trends of today are having substantial impacts on companies and workers and how they come together. They helped to break, or were influenced by the break in, the in-the-office, one-manager, nine-to-five model. That job, while it still technically exists, is a relic of a world we don't recognize anymore. Fluid, team-based, from-anywhere, always-on work is the hallmark of the world of work today. We must continue to monitor these trends, but we must also look at the data.

CHAPTER 4

THE DATA

"In God we trust. All others must bring data."
—W. Edwards Deming

NOW THAT WE HAVE REVIEWED THE MOST IMPACTFUL TRENDS OF work today, we need to look at the biggest data sources. Patterns in data, much like consistency in trends, will help us to make more intelligent forecasts of the future. Too much of the discussion on labor, present and future, is done without, or in contrast to, the data.

What data has persisted through our last three step functions in technological change? This will be challenging as good records on labor data are tough to find. While we can't analyze too much back to the beginning of the Industrial Revolution or the emergence of electrification, we can certainly see how labor statistics moved during the LEC and the emergence of computerization.

Right from the start, the data here starts to illuminate some interesting things. We would expect the average amount of time in a job to have decreased rapidly with the end of the LEC. However, it hasn't. The average time in a job has stayed relatively stable as far back as the 1960s. The average person stays in a job about four years and pretty much always has. While younger people hop around a lot more (sorry millennial-bashers, but they don't change jobs more than the previous cohorts of the same age did) and older workers tend to stay on longer, the average remains around four years. Is that to say that the LEC was a myth? In a sense, it was a myth for the majority of workers. For some workers at some companies, the LEC was certainly true, and that work has certainly changed; but the data shows that for the labor market as a whole, few workers stayed at their companies for a lifetime.

What else will the data tell us?

Let's start with the granddaddy of all labor statistics: The Labor Force Participation Rate.

The Labor Force Participation Rate

Because of its scope, the Labor Force Participation Rate is vital to understand long-term structural changes in the labor markets. While there are many labor statistics, the total number of people who are working, divided by the total number of people who could work, seems like a good indicator of what is going on in the world of labor. This takes into account almost all factors in the labor force, from on-demand work and delayed retirement to long-term unemployment and those who have left the labor force.

We see the labor force participation rate increasing from the 1950s as women moved into employment and the baby boomer generation reached working age. The story of the Labor Force Participation Rate is a slow, steady upward march, with decreases during recessions (the gray bars), until the dotcom crash in 2000. The labor force participation rate peaked at 67.3 percent right before the tech bubble burst. From there we see a slow, steady decline turn into a precipitous plunge after the Great Recession.

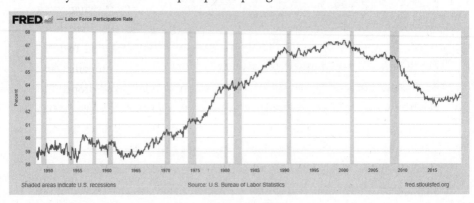

The story of the recent changes to the rate touches on many aspects of the labor force. Since the peak of labor force participation in 2000, all demographic groups have seen a decline of their respective participation rates. The biggest decline occurred in younger workers, which coincided with an increase in school enrollment. The retirement of the baby boomers also greatly impacted the overall decline in the Labor Force Participation Rate. This long-term and powerful trend was only slightly mitigated by a delay in retirement, as workers struggle with adequate retirement savings. Another demographic group greatly impacting the decline is the long-term trend of twenty-five- to fifty-four-year-olds without college degrees dropping out of the labor force. This coincides with a decrease in manufacturing employment and a corresponding increase in disability claims. This provides a challenging signal for the future of labor. Mid-career, low-skilled workers are the first to feel the effects of change as they have the least bargaining power. Their skills diminish or are not needed, and our society does not have the right incentives or structures in place to retrain them, so they drop out of the labor force.

This one chart shows us some powerful trends that will clearly impact the future, including delayed retirement and the impact of diminishing skills.

Let's examine more trend lines.

Hours Worked

Hours worked is one of the least-analyzed labor metrics, but its steady decline since the Industrial Revolution is unmistakable. *The Economist* notes that in 1870, as the Industrial Revolution was in full swing, work generally clocked in at sixty to seventy hours per week, or over three thousand hours per year. As labor unions and regulation combined to mollify the tremendous imbalance in relative power between companies and workers that the Industrial Revolution brought, hours worked dropped to the more standard model of today: forty hours of work per week, or two thousand hours per year.

The more recent past has seen much slower declines, with tremendous variation by industry and by country. According to the Organization for Economic Co-operation and Development (OECD), most industrial

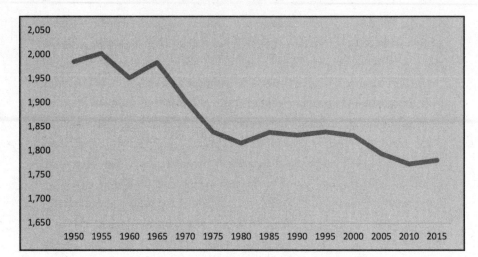

countries today are averaging about 1,750 hours per year. In the US, this number has been relatively stable since the end of the LEC in the late 1970s, as you can see from the chart below showing the average number of hours worked by year in the US.

The stability in the US could be an example that indicates the future of labor; conversely, we could look to Germany and France, where in the OECD study hours worked per year continue to fall, to 1,400 and 1,500 respectively. Could a more powerful union system and a more generous welfare state in those countries be a model as we think toward the future? Do rising standards of living mean that workers will always make the trade-off for fewer hours in the office? Do people just work until they hit a certain standard of living to be comfortable and then opt for leisure and family time? These questions are all pertinent as we think about the future of labor. What is clear is that the historic trend has veered toward fewer and fewer hours worked.

This data set is the most powerful example we have of how data persisted through our three step functions. Each change brought continued downward pressure on the number of hours worked. It should be noted that this downward movement corresponds with a clear increase in the standard of living. This decrease of hours worked and increase in standard of living is clear through every change in technology. Increases in productivity mean fewer hours of work are needed to create the average standard of living, and that average standard of living keeps getting better and better. In other words: work less, have more. This is a good data trend for workers, companies, and society.

Union Membership Rates

Union membership is a key data set and one we can get a good sense of through the different technology changes of work. With the beginning of mechanization, unions did not exist. As we discussed earlier, the abuse of power by companies and urbanization helped create the union movement.

Unions really took off after New Deal legislation put real political and legislative power behind the movement. Since a spike after the Second World War, unions have been in long-term decline. This decline would be even more dramatic if we removed public sector workers from the data as they have much higher and more stable union membership rates than workers in the private sector. Public workers have remained relatively constant at approximately 35 percent union membership. The above chart is for all workers, but private sector workers' union membership rates are now approaching just 5 percent of all employees. The most recent declines are driven mostly by new workers not joining unions, as the number of union workers in America has remained relatively constant at around fifteen million workers.

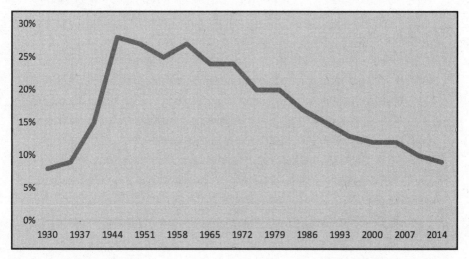

We see union membership rise during the end of the mechanization phase of technological change. But it hit a peak at around 10 percent of the labor force until the New Deal, signaling the power of economic shocks to drive legislative changes that greatly altered the landscape. While there is a clear data pattern of union membership declining during computerization, this was coupled with globalization and shareholder capitalism.

This is all the more interesting as the sentiment (the public's favorability) toward unions hits an all-time high recently. People are favorably disposed to unions but not joining them. What role will unions play in the age of robots? Will a new economic shock drive more legislative change to benefit unions? Have unions achieved the majority of their aim in an industrial world and need to be refashioned for a digital one? Will the rise of robots lead union membership to rise as workers band together to resist the job losses that may come? Much remains to be seen.

Demographics

There is no more powerful data set than demographics and how the makeup of a population drives labor. Demographics are destiny. The data in the United States (and for most industrialized countries) is clear. People are living longer. Birth rates are low and/or falling below the replacement level (2.1 births per woman where population levels are stable). This is leading to an older population and a decrease in the size of the labor force. That has already occurred with shrinking working age populations in Japan, Germany, France, and China to name a few. The United States is not far behind.

The impacts to the future of work will be vast. Older populations will result in delayed retirement, decreased dependency ratios (those who work compared to those who need social welfare), increases in social spending (Social Security and Medicare), and changes in education to incorporate more lifelong learning as older workers need to reskill.

Has the Labor Force Participation Rate found a new normal at 63 percent as baby boomers retire? Is 63 percent sustainable with increased social spending? Will working hours continue to decline as older workers choose to work less? How will robots impact one of the industries expected to create the most jobs in the future: elder care? What public policy responses will be needed to address delayed retirement and increased social spending? No conversation about the future of work can ignore demographic data.

A Look at the On-Demand Economy

There is plenty of data on the on-demand economy, and much of it is contradictory. We will look at several data sources that paint different pictures of the on-demand economy, its size, and how it has grown. We will start with tax filings.

Tax Filings

Payments to freelancers (only one part of the on-demand economy) are recorded to the IRS under tax form 1099-MISC. The number of 1099s filed is shown below.

This chart shows pronounced growth in 1099s since the Great Recession. However, it's difficult to draw too many conclusions. Did the percentage of the labor force working as freelancers also explode? What drove this increase? The increase seems to be driven by "moonlighters," those with full-time jobs who do some side work on platforms such as Uber, Lyft, and Handy. It's estimated that Uber alone issues one million 1099s to its drivers per year (although many spend their entire working day as a freelancer for Uber).

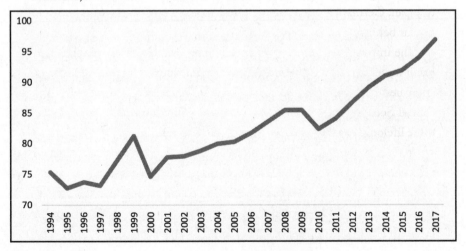

The increase in 1099s may also reflect on-demand workers doing more jobs for more customers. Has the on-demand economy increased if a given freelancer now has ten clients instead of having five last year? The number of 1099s he or she received may have doubled, but that doesn't suggest structural change in the workforce.

There is also the trend of individuals using gig platforms to hire other individuals for tasks. Companies like TaskRabbit, Fiverr, and Rover have become commonplace in many cities. To an extent, these platforms are taking work done in the gray market (running errands, housekeeping, or dog walking) and bringing them into the formal economy. Prior to Rover, people may have paid their dog walkers in cash, with no 1099 filed. Now through Rover, the dog walker is issued a 1099, and all data and payments are tracked. While there's no structural change in the way people work and no increase in the on-demand economy, this creates a new 1099 data point.

We don't have much data on the temp market, but we do have survey data on the size of the on-demand labor market as a whole.

The Surveys

Three groups have done large surveys of the on-demand labor market: MBO Partners, Upwork/Freelancers Union, and McKinsey. MBO Partners, Upwork, and the Freelancers Union provide services or software to the on-demand market, and McKinsey is a global consulting firm.

The amazing team at MBO produces the longest-running annual survey of on-demand workers in the US and covers data from approximately sixteen thousand workers. The most recent survey found that approximately 27 percent of the labor force—forty-two million people—are Independent Workers (similar to our definition of on-demand). In doing this survey since 2010, they have found that the on-demand labor force has roughly remained the same size.

For several years Upwork, the world's largest labor marketplace, and the Freelancers Union, a pioneer in on-demand worker advocacy, surveyed some six thousand Independent Workers (again, similar definition to that of our on-demand cohort) in the US. This report finds that fifty-seven million workers—about 37 percent of the labor force—are independent. Their study has the broadest definition of independent, including anyone who spends any time working outside a W-2 context, and thus produces the largest number. Their first survey in 2014 found an on-demand workforce of approximately fifty-four million. A growth of three million workers, or about 6 percent, is clearly a lot, but taken over a five-year period, hardly suggests a structural change in the labor force.

What's clear from those two long-running studies is that there is no data to support a huge increase in the number of people working on-demand. We see data indicating a slow rise, but not much else.

The McKinsey Global Institute conducted an in-depth study of employers and workers in 2016, which included a survey of eight thousand workers across the globe. They found that between 20 and 30 percent of the workforce is agile (again, similar to our definition of on-demand), representing between thirty-one to forty-six million workers in the US.

In these three surveys, we find different definitions and a range of the size of the on-demand labor force in the US, but nothing that indicates a structural change is afoot in the labor markets. Rather, we see an important segment of the labor force that is growing slightly. This stands in contrast to 1099 data—or does it? Let's look at more government data to see what else we find.

The US Bureau of Labor Statistics

The US Department of Labor through the Bureau of Labor Statistics (BLS) tracks several aspects of the labor force, and here again we find conflicting statistics about the on-demand market. We see the number of people who hold multiple jobs has declined from about 6 percent to about 5 percent over the last twenty-five years. Maybe moonlighters are not a huge growth engine of the on-demand market?

We also see that the number of people who identify as self-employed has also dropped: from 8 percent to 7 percent over the last fifty years. Maybe workers in the on-demand world don't see themselves as self-employed? Does someone who drives all day for Uber think of himself as self-employed? We may not be able to answer those questions, but we do see single-digit numbers that don't move much over long periods.

The BLS has also surveyed the on-demand market on two occasions, in 2005 and 2018. The BLS found the agile workforce (again, a similar definition to our on-demand) to have decreased slightly from 14.8 percent in 2005 to about 14 percent of the labor force, or 22.4 million workers in 2018. I will note that BLS surveys focus on primary employment and leave out the moonlighters, a very important part of the on-demand labor force.

The BLS survey also found minimal age, demographic, and educational differences in the agile workforce versus the full-time labor force. However, not surprisingly, they also found that agile workers were less likely to have health care (70 percent to 84 percent) and retirement savings (20 percent to 50 percent) than full-time employees.

One of the most consistent data points across all the studies and surveys is the satisfaction that on-demand workers have with their work arrangements. Each report found between 75 and 80 percent of workers were happy, many saying they would not take a full-time job if offered. This is interesting, but also must be taken in the context of the longest economic expansion in the nation's history. I am not sure how this survey result will change as we enter a different part of the economic cycle.

What can we conclude from the data? First, changes in the labor market don't move that quickly. Data trends are slow and steady, and those analysts that predict sea changes in the labor market are rarely correct. We see that on-demand labor has been a large part of the workforce for some time and that workers there are mostly happy with their work arrangements.

For the labor market as a whole we see clear and consistent trends around decreases in working hours, decreases in union membership, increases in standards of living, and the impacts of demographics on the Labor Force Participation Rate. Again, slow and steady movement seems to be the hallmark of labor data.

Now let's examine how companies make decisions on the labor force, as companies are the largest buyers of labor, and the supply-and-demand imbalance almost always leaves companies with the power in the labor markets.

CHAPTER 5

THE LABOR EQUATION

"Pure mathematics is, in its way, the poetry of logical ideas."
—Albert Einstein

HAVING REFLECTED ON THE HISTORY OF WORK AND ANALYZED THE current landscape, we can turn our attention to corporate decision-making in order to lay the foundations for understanding the future of work. Given that companies are the main buyers of labor, how do they choose which labor resource to use? How do they decide the makeup of their labor resource mix? As we have discussed previously, that mix can include full-time employees, part-time employees, temps, and freelancers. Which labor resource is optimal for each of the functions a company must perform?

Before we begin our exploration, we should start with *the* seminal paper on the labor market. In 1937, Nobel Laureate Professor Ronald Coase wrote a paper called "The Nature of the Firm." In this paper, he laid out his theory on why companies had come to exist and what the optimal structure was for these entities. Coase concluded that it's more efficient to have employees on hand to perform tasks, despite occasional low utilization rates, than to negotiate agreements with outside parties to perform those tasks. The outside parties are what we would call on-demand labor. Coase observed:

> The operation of a market costs something and by forming an organization and allowing some entity...to direct the resources, certain marketing costs are saved.

The "market" Coase is referring to is the on-demand labor market and the "marketing costs" represent the finding, verifying, engaging, managing, paying, and rating of that on-demand labor. By engaging full-time employees, a company has the ability to control those employees and can avoid the costs of constantly going to the "market." Of course, the hiring of full-time employees has its own inefficiencies. As Coase put it:

> A point may be reached where the costs of organizing an extra transaction with the firm are equal to the costs involved in carrying out the transaction in the open market.

In plain English, companies have employees because the transaction costs of engaging on-demand workers every time a need arises are too expensive. While Coase's theoretical ideal was that firms would have a small fixed-cost center, with most other functions procured "on-demand," Coase deemed this impractical due to transaction costs. Companies are better off with fixed-cost, full-time employees that they can control.

Coase identified three types of transaction costs in the engagement of labor. The first is search costs, or the friction of finding the right talent. The second is coordination costs, which are the costs of getting that talent to work together. Finally, we have contracting costs, meaning the friction of negotiating the how/where/what of talent work. Search, coordination, and contracting costs were very burdensome, and a company would grow its full-time labor force until bearing these costs in the market (on-demand labor) was economically beneficial.

But Coase was writing in 1937. Businesses then would have had to drive the search, coordination, and contracting costs with newspaper ads, in-person interviews, mailing letters, and tons of paperwork. Under these circumstances, is it any wonder that Coase concluded that businesses were better off paying higher fixed costs even though they would often have underutilized resources?

With the technologies that have evolved since "The Nature of the Firm" was written, it's time to revisit the math and logic behind Coase's model. The internet, mobile communications, powerful search functions, algorithms, and online marketplaces for on-demand labor all change the equation. All these factors, and many more, combine to help lower the search, coordination, and contracting costs of engaging an on-demand workforce. With these technologies taking the friction out of the process of locating and engaging on-demand resources, businesses can now cost-effectively implement Coase's theoretical ideal. That theoretical ideal is the agile corporation.

There are several factors that companies take into account when deciding on their labor resource mix and which resource gets allocated to a specific task. I call this combination of factors (and the math inherent therein) the Labor Equation. Whether implicitly or explicitly, companies are making their labor decisions based on this equation. The variables in the Labor Equation include:

- The level of intellectual property involved—how much of a company's trade secrets or intellectual property (IP) do you want to put into the hands of non-employees?
- Customer touch points—if this worker is in front of your customer often, will an on-demand worker represent the company well?
- Complexity of process—is the project too complex to explain in a scope of work to an on-demand resource?
- Integration with other work and teams—will an on-demand resource know how to navigate the company and work with other teams?
- Length of project—will it span a few hours, weeks, or several years?
- Repeatability of project—is it a one-off project or a core function?
- Ramp-up time—can someone start immediately, or do they need to be trained?
- Institutional knowledge—will the work result in building understanding or relationships that will benefit the company in the future?
- Cost—what is the all-in price, including benefits, office space, and so forth?

▶ Regulations—what do statutes and case law say about control and dependence in that industry, in that function, and in that jurisdiction?

Each company weighs these factors differently. In fact, different departments within a company will weigh these factors differently and each has very different Labor Equation calculations.

Together, HR, business units, legal departments, and executive staff conduct a careful examination of trade-offs around these factors to determine the best choice for a particular work stream: whether freelancer, temp, or W-2 workforce. Some tasks require a lot of customer touch points, heavy interaction with the rest of the team, access to loads of intellectual property, long ramp-up times, and yearlong timelines. Those are clear jobs for an employee. However, for a discrete design project with no further work, a freelancer would be great.

But there are other, more subtle variables to consider in the Labor Equation. These include how much contact the worker would have with customers, whether the company wants to "own" those interactions, how much the worker would have access to sensitive company and client data, and whether or not the worker interacts heavily with other parts of the business. These factors help drive the determination of Employee, Temp, or Freelancer as well.

And then the biggest question of all is regulatory. Before deploying resources for a project or ongoing task, today's companies must consider the regulatory aspects of their options for getting work done. All the economic factors may point to a freelancer, but if the regulatory aspect points to an employee, the company will usually pick the employee. This is about risk of misclassifying a worker. The fines and penalties for falling afoul of a state or federal labor guideline can be enormous. Companies like Microsoft, FedEx, Lowe's, and Netflix have had headlines with tens or hundreds of millions in fines.

The analyses that the Labor Equation requires, along with everything else that all companies either implicitly or explicitly do, are part of the reason why there are rarely massive movements in the size of various aspects of the labor force. Companies do not make changes quickly and do not make changes without analysis. That analysis, in the Labor Equation, really hasn't changed. In a sense, Coase's work was an expression of the Labor Equation. Thus, the labor market remains slow-moving. No CEO is coming into a meeting telling her team, "Hey, have you heard of Uber? We can use that same approach with our workforce. Let's get the transformation done by next quarter."

The Risk versus Cost Continuum

Many people believe companies make decisions based on cost and cost alone. Of course, cost is one component, but there are many other factors involved in companies' decision-making both in the near and long term. Let's look at cost through the lens of the Labor Equation. In the Labor Equation context, cost becomes a continuum, with high-risk, low-cost freelancers on one end and low-risk, high-cost full-time employees on the other end.

On this continuum, the highest-cost worker is a full-time W-2 employee (because of the benefits burden and costs associated with hiring/firing). A temp employee is slightly more expensive than an employee (due to fees you pay to the temp agency, and keep in mind that the worker is a W-2 of the temp agency so all benefits and payroll taxes are still charged) but hiring a temp does provide some flexibility. If the company decides

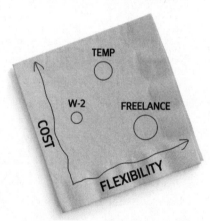

it doesn't need that temp anymore, they can just tell the temp to go. No need for severance or a lengthy termination process, just a simple "no need to show up tomorrow." The least costly worker is a freelancer as companies only need to pay them for the specific amount of work that's required, effectively giving the company a 100 percent utilization rate of this worker.

Many people believe a freelance worker is 20–30 percent less expensive because the company does not have to pay benefits. I have never seen this in the data. What we know is that freelancers still have to pay unincorporated business tax, Social Security tax, and provide for their own health care and retirement. Freelancers tend to incorporate these factors into what they charge. Thus, I have generally seen the hourly cost of a freelancer equal to the hour cost of a full-time employee. The cost benefit of using freelancers is almost always due to the utilization rates, not hourly costs. A freelancer is always 100 percent utilized, because if there is no work to do, the freelancer is not engaged. Full-time employees, however, are rarely 100 percent utilized.

But on the risk part of this continuum, the picture changes. A W-2 employee is the lowest risk. OSHA, workers' compensation insurance, disability insurance…a host of regulations and social safety net provisions protect the worker—and the company. Companies don't have to worry about a legal challenge to whether they're misclassifying that person—or the fines that can result from such a challenge.

The temp model is less risky than working with freelancers, and riskier than using W-2 employees. The big risk is a challenge to *how* a company utilizes that worker. If a company is using temps to avoid making workers their own W-2 employees for an extended period (months or even years), they run the risk of a co-employment claim. If there's a co-employment finding—meaning, if a regulatory agency finds that person is also the company's employee as well as the temp agency's employee—then the company needs to supplement what the agency provides so that the temp receives the same benefits (such as a 401[k]) that the company provides its own employees. Again, the temp is receiving a W-2 from the agency and thus is afforded all the protections and rights of a full-time worker, including access to unemployment, disability, and workers' comp insurance. So, with the temp model, while there's no risk of misclassification and the worker gets most of the benefits, the companies do have some risk of co-employment.

Freelancers are the lowest-cost option, but the highest risk. These workers are not covered by workers' comp. They could be construed to be the companies' employees if companies aren't careful to follow the rules. Companies will have to figure out what happens if the freelancer breaks something, gets injured, or injures someone else, as well as what kind of insurance the workers (and the company) need to carry. So, while these workers are lower cost, they carry a higher risk on a series of fronts.

Many of the factors of the Labor Equation favor hiring full-time employees, which is why most workers are, and will remain, employees. However, there's still a case for on-demand workers—and that case has existed for generations.

Coase was right—though ahead of his time and technology—in his theory that on-demand labor was key to enabling businesses to operate most efficiently. Organizations have already been persuaded—by their own experience or by studies they've read—of the benefits of an on-demand workforce; now their challenge is to figure out how to efficiently scale and manage on-demand talent within the confines of the Labor Equation.

If you could listen in on a meeting of C-suite executives at a global corporation, you'd likely hear a lively discussion about how the thriving on-demand economy will allow them to reengineer their workforce and better prepare for the future of work. Each executive will have a different perspective.

For example, the Chief Financial Officer might be grumbling about rising labor costs: "We need to transition to a flexible workforce in order to capitalize on optimal labor costs." The Chief Human Resources Officer is feeling the pressure of today's escalating talent wars: "We need new ways to access top talent in order to stay competitive." The Chief Operating Officer is interested in how new freelance management technologies will impact existing infrastructure and align with current business processes and wants clarification on which part of the organization should be in charge of hiring and managing this newly diverse workforce that encompasses freelancers, temps, and W-2 employees. The Chief Legal Officer is concerned about remaining compliant with federal and state labor laws. The Chief Executive Officer is focused on how it all comes together to increase shareholder value.

The Labor Equation and the Impact on the Future of Work

While the Labor Equation gives us insight into corporate decision-making, what does it tell us about the future of work? I believe it shows us that the easy transitions to on-demand have mostly been made. Where the Labor Equation dictated on-demand workforces at scale, firms did so a generation ago. Industries like field services and content creation (most workers in Hollywood are freelancers) are dominated by agile corporations. New technology has helped to bend the Labor Equation but not fundamentally change it. The Labor Equation has not changed and may never fundamentally change. Each variable may have different levels of importance to the outcome, but the largest variable—regulation—will not be changing significantly anytime soon.

However, as the world of labor evolves, companies' ability to control the variables of the Labor Equation may start to influence how we work. If a company can be sure of certain rules being followed, they can be comfortable that the regulatory risk in the Labor Equation is being minimized. By way of example, let's talk about a large media company I have worked with at WorkMarket.

This company has thousands of writers who produce content for their publications. All those writers are freelancers. The Labor Equation dictated that these writers should be freelancers, but regulatory concerns were raised. This company got comfortable with a freelance model for this work stream two decades ago, but only because the legal department set a function limit of fifty-two articles per year per freelancer. While this guideline may seem arbitrary, it was based on their analysis of the labor laws in the state where they do business, and it gave them comfort that these workers were freelancers as long as they followed that rule.

Their legal department did training session after training session and issued memo after memo making sure people knew to not issue fifty-three assignments to one writer in any one-year period. And who wants to guess how many times that rule got broken? Every single day.

The guideline was effectively useless because there was no system to track how many assignments a worker got! Only at the end of a year, when issuing IRS Form 1099-MISC, did the company account for the number of assignments. Panic ensued, as did a huge increase in the perceived risk of regulatory action. This led to legal and HR insisting that no other areas of the company could use freelancers.

The company only achieved 100 percent compliance with its legal department's guidelines when it started using WorkMarket enterprise software. WorkMarket enables companies to efficiently and compliantly organize, manage, and pay their freelancers. The software has clear limit functions that legal could calibrate for fifty-two assignments per year, preventing the overuse of freelancers.

Adopting software that enables companies to use freelancers with confidence is likely to drive an increase in the on-demand economy. Companies can now have legal, procurement, and HR departments set the guardrails and know they are being followed. This adherence helps bend the Labor Equation. While Freelance Management System (FMS) software is still not widespread, adopted in approximately 10 percent of the Fortune 500, those are the companies that are using freelancers at scale, so the impact of FMS on the on-demand economy is powerful.

In our example, the adherence to the fifty-two-assignment rule meant this customer's legal department got comfortable with the increased use of freelancers throughout the company. The Labor Equation itself is immutable, but the ability to influence some of the factors remains. By influencing their confidence in the regulatory variable of the Labor Equation, this company expanded their use of on-demand labor and helped show us a path for the future of labor.

We can use the logic of the Labor Equation and historic data patterns to gain confidence that the future of labor will not include a huge increase in actual on-demand workers.

The Labor Equation is another powerful trend that persists. Going back to Coase and his paper, "The Nature of the Firm," all the research points to a complex decision-making process by employers that has remained through all changes in the labor market. There is no reason to think the Labor Equation will not hold as we enter this next step function of technological change.

While we have overcome the technological hurdles to implement an agile business model, companies are still struggling with the legacy of a complicated regulatory framework designed for an earlier age. So now let's dig deeper into the most complex and vexing subject in the world of labor: regulation.

CHAPTER 6

THE REGULATORY QUESTION

"If you have ten thousand regulations
you destroy all respect for the law."
—Winston Churchill

THE LABOR EQUATION SHOWS US THAT REGULATION IS A KEY DRIVER OF decision-making and thus a powerful factor in thinking about the future of work. As we discussed in the history of work, regulation is also a key factor in the power balance between companies and workers. By establishing the rules of engagement to ensure fairness and by providing a safety net to ensure stability, the regulatory framework is vital for both parties to operate.

Our step functions, by imbuing more power in companies, created negative implications for workers. Society tends to eventually respond with changes to regulation, the government (or social) safety net, and tax policy. All parties have to work together to agree on new definitions of what's fair as well as manage the balance of protections and benefits that respects both the employers' need for certainty and also the workers' rights to humane treatment and fair pay.

In analyzing today's labor regulations, we find a complex web of laws that is at the center of the fabric of our society. The laws governing how we work impact every aspect of our lives from parental leave and childcare to education, training, and health care. From unemployment and disability until retirement, labor laws are with us from cradle to grave. Because this regulatory construct is so vast and far-reaching, any change to labor regulations can have far-reaching impacts to our society. This is why massive changes to regulation tend to occur only after tremendous economic shocks.

The New Deal, which is the single biggest change to occur to our labor laws, was only possible because of the devastation wrought by the Great Depression. Times of immense income inequality and social crises tend to galvanize society into bringing the labor market more into balance. Might the increase in inequality and the beginning of the fourth technological step function indicate that we may be at such a time of disruption today?

Topics such as a Universal Basic Income (or UBI, where the government pays each person a standard amount each month), government-run health care, or free college tuitions may seem implausible to many. However, think about how such concepts as social security and unemployment insurance must have seemed to people in the US in the 1920s. I am sure many thought such policies couldn't come to be, but now, can we imagine our society without them?

As mentioned earlier, many of today's labor laws and regulations are more than a hundred years old and were crafted in response to very different needs. Now, there are more gig workers building apps while sitting in office buildings than there are riveting bolts in steel girders that built those skyscrapers. Yet, our society is still working under a workers' compensation system that was enshrined into law a century ago.

I have never met an executive or worker who felt our labor regulatory system addressed the challenges of companies or workers today, let alone the challenges both will face tomorrow. Everyone knows that robots and AI will create even more need for an updating of labor laws. There is no shortage of voices calling for change to our antiquated labor laws—but there's no harmony on what that change should be.

Regulation Today

Let's start with the definition of an employee under the law. With countless different definitions of the term "employee" across federal and state levels, today's labor laws on worker classification can best be described as a confluence of the confusing, complex, and contradictory. Each state has its own definition of employees versus freelancers, and some states even have different definitions by different agencies within the state. As a result of this confusion, agencies, states, and courts have come up with a wide array of tests to determine whether a worker is an employee or a freelancer. That means a whole lot of rules across a whole lot of states and jurisdictions. A working relationship deemed acceptable for the Worker's Compensation board in Wisconsin might not work for the Unemployment Office in Louisiana.

The Fair Labor Standards Act's definition of employee is also a head-scratcher: "the term employee means any individual that is employed by an employer." Remember when our elementary school teachers scolded us to never define a word using the very word?

It would take hundreds of pages to list all the labor classification rules companies are subject to at the federal and state levels. Literally every state has its own classification rules. So, we'll try our best to summarize the approach companies take in classifying their workers. What is generally being asked is, "is the worker economically dependent on the company, or does the company exert operational control over the working conditions?" If the worker is economically dependent and the company exerts control, that worker is generally viewed as an employee of that company.

For temps, the classification rules are relatively simple, as the temp is receiving a W-2 from the staffing firm. However, companies want to show as much separation as possible. For example, temps use different systems, badging, and equipment than a full-time employee. Companies also want to make sure temps are not doing things that employees do, like career development or company off-sites. Some companies go so far as to forbid temps to have cake at office birthday parties. But the lines between a temp and an employee are a piece of cake compared to the lines between a freelancer and an employee.

For freelancers, defining classification is not a simple checklist, but a choice in a series of factors that follow the legendary IRS 20-Factor Test. This test examines the things an employee tends to do (go to an office, have set hours, earn benefits, have her expenses paid, receive training, use company equipment) and those that a freelancer tends to do (have profit-and-loss risk, operate as an independent company, market her skills to multiple employers, have business insurance).

The rules do not say "thou shalt do this and not that," but delineates what one classification *tends* to do.

The most recent (April 2019) of several clarifying memos from the Wage and Hour Division of the Federal Department of Labor cites recent Supreme Court precedent in highlighting the six factors used to determine economic dependence:

1) The nature and degree of the employer's control;
2) The permanency of the worker's relationship with the employer;
3) The amount of the worker's investment in facilities, equipment, or helpers;
4) The amount of skill, initiative, judgment, or foresight required for the worker's services;
5) The worker's opportunities for profit or loss;
6) The extent of integration of the worker's services into the employer's business.

However, even if all six are met, or none are met, the worker may still be found to be an independent contractor. Every circumstance, for every function, in every company, in every industry is different.

Companies I have worked with almost always cite regulatory concerns as the biggest impediment to engage more freelancers. Some companies will simply not allow any freelancers as part of their workforce. This cuts them off from an important source of talent, but the companies' fear of falling afoul of a regulation drives their decisions.

This look at worker classification underscores two important things: first, how complex, contradictory, and confusing labor laws are; second, how without change to these laws, there will be no great increase in on-demand labor. Without regulatory change, the labor market tends not to move very much.

Given the prominence of Uber and other on-demand companies, this story on worker classification has been on the front pages a lot. It has led to lots of thinking on how to reform our labor laws to address the modern world of work. I have heard ideas around a sort of middle ground between full-time employees and freelancers; a third classification alongside a W-2 and a 1099. I have seen proposals on hour-banks or pro-rata solutions, where an employee contributes payroll taxes in proportion to how many hours a week a freelancer works for them.

In my opinion, adjusting our labor laws just for on-demand would be seriously flawed. As we have shown, the on-demand market is neither new nor exploding. While there are mass changes needed to our regulatory framework for labor, those focused on on-demand would be missing the majority of challenges workers face. The struggles of the on-demand worker, while severe for many workers, is not the biggest challenge faced by workers in the power imbalance that regulation is designed to rectify.

What I believe we need is comprehensive reform that addresses the coming changes wrought by robots and AI. Our conversations on reform should include things like decoupling health care from work (the US is in the only industrialized country to pair health care to a job), changes in education and training programs, and infrastructure to allow everyone access to the benefits of a digital economy. There are numerous conversations to be had about UBI or changes to the Earned Income Tax Credit, where workers qualify for refunds of taxes paid (and is one of the largest anti-poverty programs in the US). Sadly, history has shown us that having that nuanced a conversation on something this far reaching may take an economic shock like the Great Depression.

At the heart of labor regulation is tax policy. How our government raises revenue becomes a key component of labor reform as payroll and income taxes make up about 90 percent of government tax receipts in 2018. On this front, we see technology bending the regulatory framework.

The Tax Gap

As with many things, the concern about regulation comes down to money, specifically tax revenue for states. Poorly defined categories lead employers to misclassify workers as freelancers rather than employees. I believe very few companies intentionally misclassify workers. They are doing what they think is right in the face of a complex, confusing, and contradictory tangle of regulations. State regulators are also doing their level best to help workers and ensure that as many people as possible are protected by the regulations and the social safety net. If workers are misclassified, this both cheats workers of the benefits to which they're entitled and is estimated to cost billions of dollars every year in lost federal and state tax revenue. This is due to three factors:

► Unrecorded income that independent contractors may not report;

► Independent contractors' use of social programs like unemployment even though they don't pay unemployment insurance;

► Additional tax deductions when independent contractors write off against income expenses that they would not be allowed to deduct if they were employees.

Even without regulatory changes, these gaps may be shrinking. As more work moves to on-demand platforms, the amount of unrecorded income declines. The example we discussed earlier with dog walkers is informative here. Dog walkers now have to file their earnings through Rover or Wag—it's not entirely clear how many self-reported the cash payments they received before the apps. This is a small step in the right direction.

There remains an interesting battle between the math of the Labor Equation, a company's interpretation of the regulatory environment, and the new technologies bending these equations. There is no clear path forward because clarity involves the regulatory machine at its core. We will just stumble from one mini-crisis to the next. However, what we can conclude about the future of labor, in the absence of regulatory clarity, is that it will not veer from the past too sharply.

CHAPTER 7

WHAT ON-DEMAND LABOR TEACHES US ABOUT THE FUTURE OF WORK

"Kids don't remember what you try to teach them.
They remember what you are."

—Jim Henson

WHILE I MAY ARGUE THAT ON-DEMAND LABOR IS NOT THE FUTURE OF labor, I believe that we are at the end of jobs and the rise of the on-demand worker. That rise is reflected in the tenets of the on-demand market we see permeating throughout the full-time labor force. These tenets are increasingly hitting all workers regardless of classification. I have seen it in companies both large and small. Both workers and companies would be wise to watch these trends.

On-demand labor has been around through all three step functions that have impacted the world of work. It is only fairly recently that it has become more talked about as the consumer aspect of on-demand has become a larger part of our lives through gig economy platforms such as

Uber, Lyft, and Handy. While not new, on-demand may be the tip of the spear of the changes in an ever-evolving world of work. We see throughout history that when the supply-and-demand balance favors workers, workers tend to want to work on-demand. Have you recently tried to hire a block-chain developer or a cybersecurity programmer as a full-time employee? Most won't do it. They are so in demand right now that they will only consult or work on short-term projects.

In many ways, this is just "back to the future." As I wrote earlier, prior to the Industrial Revolution, workers would usually have a portfolio of work activities. The concept of a permanent steady job only started after the rise of companies during the first industrial revolution. The modern idea of a steady job emerged only after the rise of the Lifetime Employment Contract. Although data tells us the LEC was mostly fiction, it was still an important part of the narrative of work. With the end of that narrative and the return of workers deriving their income and professional satisfaction from a portfolio of work, we are not seeing something new, but the return of what already existed, and still exists in most of the world.

What is new is the infiltration of the following tenets of the on-demand market into the full-time employment world.

► Total personal responsibility
► Task-based labor
► Data-driven HR
► Algorithms for work allocation
► Impermanence
► Platforms

Total Personal Responsibility

On-demand workers know exactly where they stand in their professional lives and are taking responsibility for their own business success, career progression, and financial security, including retirement and health care. Without a full-time employer, they only have partial access to the government safety net and have to rely totally on their individual safety net.

Whether or not on-demand work was their choice, these workers know there is no one to help them but themselves.

Full-time, W-2 employees don't have companies fully taking care of retirement anymore; defined benefit plans evolved into defined contribution plans that then became 401(k)s. Companies are contributing less and less to healthcare costs. They do less training, with some companies going so far as to ask workers to complete training on their own time. This means a company's employees today are approaching the same personal responsibility for their careers as on-demand workers. This includes the marketing of their skill sets. For on-demand workers, that means getting more jobs. For full-time workers, it means getting staffed on the right projects, working with the right teams, and advancing your career. Whether on-demand or full-time, the reality is becoming that all workers are responsible for being more entrepreneurial about their own careers.

Total personal responsibility is permeating the full-time labor market.

Task-Based Labor

One interesting ramification of the gig economy is the extent to which it has led to companies taking a task-based approach to all labor, not just the work they are putting out to freelancers. I have seen this trend at Work-Market, as more and more companies use our FMS to match the skills of their full-time workforce with applicable tasks. They're looking at their full-time jobs as a set of tasks for their W-2 employees, which is causing a subtle change in dynamic for people throughout the company.

Much like the assembly line broke down the artisan process into a series of steps, the service world is moving toward breaking projects into their component tasks. The advancement of project management software has also played a large part in the development of task-based labor. Platforms like Asana, Basecamp, Trello, and Jira make the disaggregation of work into bite-sized tasks more feasible. Freelancers are already used to this process, as working on tasks is a hallmark of the freelance economy. Work is being broken into tasks, as tasks are easier to measure and track. The trend here is becoming clearer: any work that can be broken into tasks will be.

Task-based work is permeating the full-time labor market.

Data-Driven HR

Freelancers know that they're constantly being assessed and that their performance drives decisions about whether or not a firm will use their skills for the next project. Platforms that allocate work usually track how quickly freelancers respond, their keystroke activity, the location of their phones, their deliverables, and many other data points. These data points are included in a detailed profile of the freelancer's work product and process. These data points help future employers searching profiles, or increasingly the WorkMarket algorithms, determine who the best worker is for a company's task.

As a person selecting a worker, what would you do if you saw two freelancers with similar skills: one with a 98 percent satisfaction rating, whose on-time arrival rate is 97 percent, and who completes the task 99 percent on time; the other with 73 percent, 27 percent, and 12 percent ratings, respectively? Is it really much of a choice?

Data is driving the majority of decisions in the on-demand world and is beginning to influence decisions about W-2 employees as well. HR departments are now including much more granular data in annual reviews to assess performance, both qualitatively and quantitatively, just as they would do for freelancers. This ties in well with the trend toward task-based work. Tasks are designed to be measured more closely. It's one thing to measure how a deployment of a new technology went nationwide, it's another to understand that machine 731, at location 82, for client ABC was installed on time (Monday at 7:00 a.m. the installer showed up with the right parts) and that the manager of location 82 was satisfied with the professionalism and skill of the worker who performed that task.

In fact, we are already starting to see the annual review for full-time employees give way to more frequent and project-based check-ins, and technology tools that are making more frequent review cycles possible. One of the most innovative of these platforms is StandOut. StandOut formalizes weekly priority listings, manager check-ins, and frequent pulses on engagement and performance. And StandOut is an application for full-time employees. Instead of an annual performance review with one assessment of an employee's performance (with a bias to how they did over the last few weeks!), a manager is seeing at least fifty-two data points on their performance on specific projects. StandOut is slowly replacing annual review programs, and workers are feeling more engaged as they have weekly touchpoints with a manager who now better understands their work and progress.

Soon all the data derived from tasks and more frequent touch points across platforms like these will drive decisions in the world of work.

Data-driven HR is permeating the full-time labor market.

Algorithms for Work Allocation

As companies increasingly deploy a variety of labor resources in a task-based, data-driven model, technology is going to help determine how they allocate that work.

In the on-demand world, platforms and companies use algorithms to route the tasks that they assign to freelancers. Companies set the rules, based on their interpretation of the factors in the Labor Equation, and software programs use algorithms to automatically route tasks to several freelancers to bid. The system then interprets their responses: price change requests, work availability, questions on the scope of work, etc. Based on the rules the company provided, the system selects a freelancer for the task.

Work that needs to be done ASAP gets offered first to the nearest person, based on their phone's location. Work in a school environment goes to someone who has worked in other school environments before. The more work that goes through the system, the more data the system has to make informed decisions. That's how it works in the freelance economy—and I am seeing it in every part of the labor force. Again, I am seeing companies use WorkMarket's algorithms to allocate work to their full-time employees.

As an example, I have worked with accounting and consulting firms that use our software to create profiles for all their employees with their skills and availability. Then, as new projects come in, they use our algorithms to staff the project based on need, skill, and availability. They no longer rely on a manager's knowledge of who is good at what but use a system and data to allocate more efficiently. They can also see where they may have skills gaps and recruit new resources or train their existing team to ensure they have the right skills for the work they are being asked to perform for their clients.

Algorithms allocating work are permeating the full-time labor market.

Impermanence

Perhaps the biggest difference between employees and freelancers is that freelancers know they have no job security. With the illusion of security stripped away, freelancers see their careers and their financial security more clearly than many employees. Freelancers often perceive that they have more job security than employees. Employees have a single point of failure. If something happens to their company or their function, team, or department, and they lose their job, the money stops coming in. But I see freelancers have on average fifteen customers, so they have many points of failure. During an economic downturn, their business may shrink, but it is unlikely to vanish entirely.

Today's full-time employees are adopting the same mindset, hastened by the end of the notion of the LEC. While a full-time employee does have a single point of failure, they know it's wise to be ready and looking for the next opportunity. The largest increase in the on-demand world seems to be moonlighters. These workers are diversifying their incomes (mostly due to need) and their skills to address the lack of permanence (and income inequality) in today's labor market. While the data tells us people still stay in a job for an average of four years, their approach to work has changed. I have met very few people who still believe their companies have made a lifetime commitment to them, and they have returned the favor.

Impermanence has permeated the full-time labor market.

Platforms

An increasing number of on-demand workers receive their work via a technology platform. Currently that number is between 25 and 30 percent, and it is rising rapidly. The platforms that deliver the work in the on-demand world fall into three categories: marketplaces, Vendor Management Systems (VMS), and Freelance Management Systems (FMS). Collectively these platforms are processing about $250 billion in spending in the US.

This is up from a base of zero fifteen years ago as the first VMS platforms and marketplaces were introduced.

By my last count there were 248 labor platforms operating in the world today. There are about 17 VMS platforms, with Fieldglass and Beeline IQN far and away the largest, with each processing over $20 billion in labor spending annually. There are 230 labor marketplaces; Upwork is by far the largest with nearly $2 billion in labor spending annually. Any category of labor you can think of, there is a marketplace for that: Priori Legal and Bodhala for lawyers, 99designs and Behance for designers, Handy and TaskRabbit for handymen, Rover and Wag for dog walkers—the list goes on and on. As for FMS, by my count, there is only one, WorkMarket.

The platforms allow companies to efficiently and compliantly engage an on-demand labor force. The need for the largest buyers of labor (companies) to have the right systems and processes in place was always a major impediment to the on-demand market; platforms are solving that problem.

The invention and proliferation of these platforms have helped bring organization to the previous chaos and have helped drive the growth of the on-demand economy. Companies can now manage thousands or tens of thousands of workers in an efficient way. They can also use the platforms to mitigate their risk of worker misclassification or other compliance concerns by using business rules on "Who" (the workers they use) and "How" (rules for workers engagement) they harness on-demand workers.

Marketplaces connect the buyers and the sellers of work. These allow for efficient sourcing of labor. The VMS and FMS technologies help companies efficiently and compliantly organize, manage, and pay temps and freelancers, respectively. These three software platforms are starting to converge with marketplaces developing the enterprise software tools that VMS and FMS bring. And VMS and FMS platforms are building marketplaces of workers and moving into each other's side of the on-demand world.

Some platforms are also starting to incorporate full-time workers. Again, one of the biggest use cases we have seen recently for WorkMarket is companies using our FMS to manage their full-time workers. Companies upload their full-time employees into WorkMarket's system, so they can see their workforces' skills and availability in real time and use our algorithms to staff projects.

In addition, large Human Capital Management platforms (like ADP) are building in the tools necessary for companies to manage full-time workers and on-demand workers side by side. By building on-demand-like tools, the large HCM players see how companies are starting to manage full-time workers and on-demand workers in the same task-oriented way.

Platforms are permeating the full-time labor market.

Best Practices for On-Demand Workers... Meaning *All* Workers

With the tenets of on-demand work permeating the full-time labor force, what are the best practices for success in an on-demand world? As we discussed, on-demand workers are responsible for their own development, training, marketing, and monetization of their skills. These are entrepreneurial skills that on-demand workers, and increasingly all workers, need to master to be successful:

- ► **Online networking**
- ► **Continuous investment in their own human capital**
- ► **Building their "soft" skills**
- ► **Adapting to constant change**

Online Networking

Online social networking is transforming many aspects of society, and the labor force is no exception. The impact of Facebook and Instagram may not be as clear to a professional as LinkedIn, but they are powerful cogs in today's on-demand machinery. Most people know about the practice of prospective or current employers checking employee social feeds for "negative" behavior. We have all heard some version of the tale of the worker who calls in sick yet posts a live stream of himself on a beach drinking... and gets fired the next day.

In the freelance economy, social networks are even more important. Having connections in common with prospective clients helps build trust. Common connections build an incentive alignment that helps both buyers and sellers of labor feel confident that they share a commitment to reach the best possible result—a job well done and paid on-time. People are less likely to perform poorly for someone they are connected to than for someone with whom they have no common relationships.

In the freelance economy, where work can be short-term and distributed by anonymous online profiles, the added opportunity to build trust through mutual connections can be particularly important. By mastering the online social network and building broad connections, you increase the chances that you will be connected to a future employer. The old adage of "it's not what you know, it's who you know" is even more true when you are working on-demand.

The same holds true for online platforms where you can market your skills. As discussed, there are online marketplaces for lawyers, accountants, chefs, nannies, and virtually every other profession or skill set. This level of transparency and information brings such a high level of efficiency to the on-demand world that most companies find themselves occasionally using marketplaces to find workers. This is why Upwork claims two million buyers and sixteen million workers on its platform.

Continuous Investment in Human Capital

On-demand workers learned the importance of continuous, lifelong learning a long time ago. In order to stand out from the online competition, on-demand workers need to continually invest in their own professional development, whether that be in the form of ongoing education, licenses, or certifications. From soliciting and receiving ratings and reviews for work to attending networking events and taking online classes, freelancers are always looking to ensure that their skill sets and credentials are well suited to current market demands.

Full-time "permanent" employees would do well to adopt this mindset, too. Successful people focus on building skills that have value in the market and establish a solid financial base, so they can move from one position to the next.

As algorithms take over the allocation of work, these systems are looking for hard data points to allocate tasks. Prior task completions will increase a worker's odds of being allocated a task, but so will skill certifications, license validations, and relevant trainings. The more workers can augment their human capital, the more work can be allocated to them.

Companies like Lynda.com (bought by LinkedIn for $1 billion) and Skillshare are helping workers to build their skills and enhance their job prospects. There is a reason Adecco, the largest staffing firm, bought General Assembly, one of the most common places young workers go to build their software skills. The industry for providing workers with the right skills in an ever-changing workplace is booming. It's booming because constant change, and thus reskilling, is now the norm.

This focus on continuous lifelong learning is a frequent theme in the future of work. As industries and skill needs change ever more rapidly, workers of all classifications must keep pace. They have to ensure that they have marketable skills with which they can earn a living. Everyone has to be a lifelong learner.

Building Soft Skills

Whether or not a freelancer works onsite, he still needs to demonstrate social skills such as collaboration and teamwork. Successful freelancers will be careful to cultivate their relationships with virtual teammates and to build reputations for having a professional, collegial attitude. Good people skills translate into enthusiastic ratings—and more projects.

Remember, work is increasingly being broken into tasks. Task-based work means collaboration with others as a part of a larger project. Each task may have dependencies to other tasks in the project. Those able to communicate and collaborate will have an advantage

The reality is that everyone is now in sales. Workers are selling themselves and their skills at all times. Whether it's professionalism when doing a task, collaboration and communication during a project, or professional networking, those with the right soft skills will thrive in the on-demand world.

Another benefit of soft skills building is the growing importance of "humanness" in an increasingly automated world. In all the studies on the future of work, the jobs which are least likely to be automated are the jobs focused on interaction with other humans and on those soft skills. Work based on "human" capabilities such as curiosity, imagination, creativity, and social and emotional intelligence has a higher probability of remaining nonautomated and even growing as a part of the labor force.

Adaptability to Constant Change

The only constant is change. That has never been truer, and it applies to all workers. Your projects are short-lived. Your skills will diminish. The work in an industry will disappear. But if you are ready for change and accept it as a part of the process, you can adapt. New projects will come, and every now and again one will be longer term. Your skills can constantly be refreshed and upgraded. New industries will pop up, and new opportunities will evolve.

In every interview I have done for this book, I close with this: what advice would you give to a person just entering the workforce? The answer has almost always been the same: "Be prepared for constant change."

Disadvantages of Freelancing

On-demand workers, and freelancers in particular, face challenges that full-time employees no longer face. Some of this is due to freelancing not being captured in New Deal legislation. Part of it is also that there is no union clout for on-demand workers. Despite being a large part of the labor force, there is no organizing infrastructure for the on-demand world. Representing only 10 percent of the work force today, unions still wield tremendous clout. Conversely, on-demand workers contribute 25–30 percent of the labor force and have virtually no clout.

The disadvantages of freelancing that come up the most are the lack of access to the social safety net, the fear of uncertainty, and the difficulty navigating the financial world.

The most tangible disadvantage for the freelance workforce is the fact that in the US, the social safety net is almost entirely delivered through the W-2 full-time employment model. As many as fifty million working Americans spend at least some time working outside this W-2 model and are therefore being partially shut out of the social safety net. There is no unemployment if your work streams dry up. There is no workers' compensation or disability insurance if you get hurt. Of course, these are all things that people pay for through automatic deductions from the W-2 payroll—and as a freelancer, you don't have this money coming out of your pocket every two weeks. But not enough freelancers save money for a rainy day or purchase insurance directly. Freelancers are also not covered by a host of regulations that protect full-time employees, such as minimum wage laws, discrimination laws, overtime regulation, and many more. Hopefully there is change coming in the form of better consumer-level insurance offerings or comprehensive labor reform, but we are in an era of total personal responsibility, and hope is not a strategy.

What I have seen is the advent of companies like Bunker and 1099Policy that are helping companies to get the insurance they need to work with on-demand workers. While it still ties a worker to a company (the company gets the insurance not the worker), at least it creates the protections that both companies and workers need.

And then there is the fear of uncertainty. Chances are that more people would switch to working on-demand if they could, but it is all too common for Americans to sacrifice their talents, skills, and aspirations in exchange for an uninspiring job with the security of full benefits. As a wise man once said, "The three most addictive things in life are heroin, carbs, and a monthly salary." Fear should not dictate how we live our lives. Yet, countless individuals and families do exactly this because it is their only viable means to access adequate care and peace of mind.

While the on-demand construct can be scary and competitive, we should again note that the data says that 75–80 percent of those who work on-demand are happy with their work arrangement. Many report not wanting to trade their freedom for the illusion of security that people associate with a full-time job. But *many* is not *all*.

Lastly, we have the world of finance. When you apply for a car loan, mortgage, or apartment lease, what document do lenders ask you for? A copy of your IRS Form W-2. How does one navigate this world if he doesn't have a W-2, but rather a collection of 1099s? This is a challenge, but large banks have recognized the trend. I have been advising some of the nation's largest banks who understand the challenges that freelance workers face and are trying to tailor their products (mortgages, car loans, and such) to the freelance workforce.

Another gap for freelancers in the world of finance is the payment cycle. Full-time workers know they will get paid every two weeks. They know when payday is and can plan around it. Companies very rarely miss payroll. That is not the reality a freelancer operates in. Freelancers are not paid through payroll, but through accounts payable. They are basically like any other vendor, subject to late payment, lost invoices, and getting shunted from department to department tracking down invoices. This creates a cash flow issue where freelancers can't be sure when their next check is coming.

ADP is working with several vendors and trying to bridge this gap not only for the freelance worker but also for the full-time worker who may need their money more often than the two-week pay cycle. ADP's Future of Pay initiatives should not only break the need for payday loans, but also help the freelance workforce to factor (sell) their receivables at nearly the same rates as large companies do.

Collectively, the things that work about on-demand, along with the issues with the freelance component of on-demand, are all struggles that every worker must think about. The future of labor may not be the complete Uberization of work, but the challenges of the Uber driver community are a part of our collective future of labor.

CHAPTER 8

THE FUTURE OF WORK: NEAR TERM

"The future is already here—it's just not evenly distributed."
—William Gibson

OUR AIM HAS BEEN TO LOOK AT HISTORY AND ANALYZE THE PRESENT. We are doing that through the lens of the three technological step functions that have impacted work. Examining what data and trends have persisted enables us to hold a high degree of confidence in predicting the near-term future of work. This approach has left me with four predictions about the near-term labor markets that I can make with a high degree of confidence.

These four areas are supported not only by our study of the past and the present but also the actions of corporate leaders I have met with as they prepare their companies for the future of work. I believe the near-term future of work will incorporate:

- ▶ Convergence of on-demand and full-time workers
- ▶ Only incremental changes to the labor force
- ▶ Alumni Labor Clouds
- ▶ Total Talent Management

These first two, convergence and incremental change, we have touched on before, but Alumni Labor Clouds and Total Talent Management are new concepts we will unpack.

Convergence

Though I have called this book *The End of Jobs*, I hope I have explained well enough that jobs will not end—very far from it. The concept of a job is safe and sound for the near and medium term (nothing is safe in the long term). The amount of time we are working will continue to decline as it has for centuries and the on-demand labor force will continue to grow slowly as it has for the last few decades. However, Coase's model and the Labor Equation will continue to hold, and there will always be a benefit to companies having full-time employees. It's the context in which those employees operate that will change.

As we think about how workers in an on-demand model have persisted through three step functions of change and how workers in an on-demand model function today, we are seeing the future: the convergence of the full-time labor market and the on-demand model. Over the last few decades, full-time workers are inching ever closer to on-demand workers in how they view work, how they approach work, and how they are treated and managed at work. This trend, the convergence of full-time and on-demand labor, is a powerful force in the future of work.

I see it every day in the continued chipping away of the corporate safety net and the increase in total personal responsibility. The defined benefit pension plan becomes a defined contributed plan becomes a 401(k) becomes an IRA. Healthcare costs continue to rise, with most of the increased burden being put on workers. Training and development are increasingly being pushed onto full-time employees. These are all the realities of on-demand labor, and as they continue to permeate the full-time labor force, there will be convergence on total personal responsibility for all workers. Even with data showing the LEC as more myth than fact, the idea of any worker solely relying on a company for their retirement, health care, and training and development is becoming pure fiction.

While there are examples today of companies like Starbucks and Amazon offering to pay for college and companies like Walmart increasing wages across the nation, these are exceptions. I would also argue that these changes are more a factor of a tight labor market toward the end of an economic expansion than a new trend among companies. Let's see what companies do as the labor market slackens during the next cycle.

I also see convergence in the atomizing of work into projects and tasks. I see convergence in the use of algorithms in the workplace. I see convergence in more and more data being captured on employees. The annual review becomes quarterly plans becomes monthly goals becomes weekly check-ins. I see the large HR software players for full-time employees evolving their software solutions so that companies can capture more data on workers, manage teams, and manage tasks. I see these systems incorporating advanced AI to assist in the hiring and staffing decisions. With the realities of on-demand work permeating the full-time labor force, there is a convergence of labor.

This convergence may in effect be a good thing for all workers. Remember, 75–80 percent of on-demand workers are happy due to the flexibility and empowerment they have. Remember that, collectively, we are spending fewer and fewer hours at work.

Given the data and trends, we can have a high degree of confidence in the prediction of a future of work that incorporates the convergence of full-time workers and on-demand workers.

The Rise of On-Demand Workers is nearly completed.

Incremental Changes

As we have seen, data in the labor market moves slowly. The slow movements are generally driven by the Labor Equation and the analytical approach companies use in making workforce planning decisions. The average tenure in a job has stayed almost constant for seventy years. The on-demand market has grown very slowly for a generation or two. The total number of hours worked per year has fallen, but it has taken decades to get a 10 percent decline. The Labor Force Participation Rate moves less than 0.2 percent a year in the vast majority of years.

When changes do come at a rapid pace, they come due to regulatory reform, social changes, or economic shocks. We saw large movements in union membership after the New Deal. We saw relatively big increases in the Labor Force Participation Rate after women could more readily enter the workforce. Income inequality spikes with changes to the tax code. Economic shocks like the Great Depression or the Great Recession can also cause rapid movements in the labor markets. Not only through the economic shocks do we see impact on employment, but also through changes in regulation. The most powerful example is the economic imbalances and income inequality of the Great Depression fueling society's need for the New Deal.

Demographic shifts can also cause large changes in labor statistics, but they are hardly rapid changes. Demographic changes take a generation to hit the labor market. No one was surprised that the baby boom generation turned eighteen and started to enter the labor force, causing the slow and steady increase in the Labor Force Participation Rate. Much like no one is surprised by the slow and steady decline of the Labor Force Participation Rate as the baby boomers begin to retire.

For the most part though, we should be skeptical when someone says things like "on-demand is going to rise from 30 percent to 50 percent of the labor force in ten years." Is it possible? Of course. It's just unlikely unless we are also predicating a large regulatory change that would alter the Labor Equation. While technology can help bend the Labor Equation, only fundamental regulatory, social, or demographic change will alter the underlying math.

I am also not sure what social norms may change that would impact labor statistics, at least in the Western world. There may be changes to how the workplace views the formerly incarcerated, the long-term unemployed, or those on long-term disability. These groups entering the labor force en masse could effect reasonably large change, but each only represents about 1 percent of the labor force. Thus, the changes, while good for society, do not auger large statistical movements in the labor force.

Movements in the labor market have been slow and steady, and absent any economic shock, they will most likely remain slow and steady.

Alumni Labor Clouds

What is increasingly clear is that every company faces a series of challenges in the near term: (i) a skills gap as demographics and other forces drive a tighter labor market; (ii) retiring workers walking out the door with tremendous institutional, customer, and technical knowledge, which is becoming more pronounced due to the 10,000 baby boomers who retire every day; and (iii) with the average tenure in a job stable at four years, staff turnover averages around 25 percent.

The solution to these challenges is that most companies will start engaging more closely with their alumni, in what are known as Alumni Labor Clouds (ALC). An ALC is created when a worker moves into either Retired or Voluntary Departure status in a company system (there are generally three other statuses: Active, Involuntary Departure [fired], and Deceased), at which time their data is automatically (with their approval due to privacy regulations) moved into a new system. That system takes all their employment data and augments (with the former employee's input) the profile on that employee with their skills, projects, customers, and other information relevant to the company. Now each former employee has a robust profile that the former company can access.

The former company can use this cloud of former employees for several things. First, they can rehire those former employees for existing roles. The cost of rehiring an old employee is a fraction of what it costs to find someone new. Second, they can engage that former worker as a temp (for seasonal needs) or as a freelancer (for task-based work). Third, they can solicit this pool of former colleagues for referral and lead generation on new hires or clients.

Having trouble with the XYZ technology or system but no one at your company remembers how it was built? Bring back three of the team members who worked on it but are now retired for a three-week consulting assignment. Need to engage five thousand workers for the holiday rush at all your stores? You could pay a staffing firm a markup to find those five thousand, or you can keep in touch with all the workers who worked with you the last few years and engage them directly, saving millions in staffing firm fees. Want to hire someone with a rare skill set in Minneapolis and are having trouble finding that person? Send an assignment to all your former teammates in Minnesota with a $5,000 bounty to anyone who can recommend a great person. The company is able to more efficiently find workers, and workers (and retirees) are able to earn money and stay engaged—it's truly a win-win.

In the near term most companies with greater than a few hundred employees will have a system for staying in touch with their former colleagues, to everyone's benefit.

Total Talent Management

The future will also embrace a Total Talent Management (TTM) approach to corporate labor resource planning. TTM incorporates the trends we've been discussing in this book: convergence, task-based work, algorithms allocating work, data-driven HR, and agile teams. These come together across all labor resources to ensure companies can allocate the right labor resource with the right skills and availability to the tasks that need to be completed.

TTM is the idea that a company can manage all their labor resources in one place—with full-time employees, part-time employees, temporary employees, freelancers, vendors, robots, drones, and so on, all in one database. With TTM, companies can take a broad view of all labor resources, including the skills and availability of anyone (or thing) that can perform a task. Companies can then compare their labor resources against their needs and plan accordingly. TTM also allows companies to fully incorporate on-demand workers (and other labor assets) side by side with their full-time employees.

TTM looks like this:

Step 1

Work is broken into tasks or projects. As we discussed, this is a powerful trend permeating the full-time workforce.

Step 2

Those tasks are analyzed by an algorithm in order to staff the right agile teams with the right skills (hard and soft) and availability to perform the task. The algorithms are populated with data based on the company's Labor Equation. What are the preferences or business needs by geography, customer, or other variables? What are the regulatory guidelines in that jurisdiction? Those are fed into the AI system, which learns from each interaction how to optimize for the desired business outcomes by task. Sometimes you optimize for speed, sometimes for profit, sometimes for training.

Step 3

The AI system matches the task against a Labor Plane. The Labor Plane is another AI system that houses all worker profiles and data. These are all resources that the company works with: its full-time employees, part-time employees, temp workers, freelancers, robots, drones, AI systems, and vendors. Each resource in the Labor Plane is tracked on their skills, the quality of their work, with whom they work well, their availability, their professionalism, and a host of other labor statistics. The Labor Plane is always thinking and will let a company know where there are gaps in availability or skills. The appropriate training modules can be assigned, or new resources can be recruited into the Labor Plane. Thus, the Labor Plane is always ready with the resources necessary to staff the tasks the company usually needs.

Step 4

An agile team is selected from the Labor Plane to perform the task, and all relevant information is passed to the team. Workers will be on multiple agile teams on any given moment working with other workers of their classification (freelancers working with freelancers) or working across labor classifications (two freelancers, three vendors, a robot, six temps, and three full-time employees working on a project together). The team works together in one system to communicate and upload components of the task. The system is tracking their responsiveness, collaboration, and delivery times. Once the task is completed, the work is submitted for processing.

Step 5

All the data that is captured on how the team performs, including "Uber-like" ratings (by those for whom they did the work) flows back to each worker's profile on the Labor Plane. Signals are sent to other systems like accounting (to bill a client for the work completed), Accounts Payable (to pay any freelancers on the project), and a Project Management software (to aggregate the task into an end product).

This is the future of work. This is a company using technology to balance labor with the work, or tasks, that need to be completed. This is how companies are using data, mobile, machine learning, APIs, algorithms, and AI to optimize their workforce. This is how companies can operate in a flexible, agile structure and compete in any economic environment.

The Rise of Agile Companies is at hand.

Imagine a world where the following happens: a machine connected to the Internet of Things (IoT) sends a signal that it needs repair. That signal goes into project management software that creates a task to be performed: fix Machine #731 located at 123 Main Street. That task is compared to the available resources in your Labor Plane with the skills to fix a machine like #731. The software determines that no full-time employees are in the area and that it would take too long to spin up a temp worker; so, it sends the task to five freelancers who are in the area with the right skills, insurance, and licenses to perform that work. Since 123 Main Street happens to be a government office, the system also looks for someone with the right background check and drug test (that government client requires all workers to be drug and background checked, and the algorithm knows this).

The system offers the freelancers a price for the task, determined by looking at the market price for all similar tasks in the same area. Three respond that they can fix Machine #731 in the next hour, but two ask for more money. The algorithm selects the third worker who was willing to take the market price and assigns her the task. She is dispatched to the site; her mobile phone automatically checks her in when she arrives at 123 Main Street. As she had the right skills, she fixes Machine #731 quickly and with no issues. Machine #731 confirms that it is now functioning properly, triggering the automatic production of an invoice for the task. The invoice is sent via API to the accounting software, which instructs the bank to pay the freelancer. Data on the task, her responsiveness, and her skills is sent back to her profile on the Labor Plane.

That's Total Talent Management in action. The surprising part of all this is not the speed or efficiency, or that the only human involved is the woman who fixed Machine #731, but that it currently happens thousands of times a day. Service companies using WorkMarket software coupled with ADP's next generation HR Platforms are currently managing all their labor assets in one plane and using AI to automate selection of labor resources and management of tasks.

The future is already here.

CHAPTER 9

THE RISE OF THE MACHINES

"Judgment Day is inevitable."
—Arnold Schwarzenegger as The Terminator

WITH OUR NEAR-TERM CONCLUSIONS OUT OF THE WAY, WE CAN FOCUS on the long term. And there is only one thing people want to know about the long-term future of work…the robots! So, let's discuss our impending Judgment Day, when the robots take over.

As I have said many times in this book, we stand at the precipice of the fourth step function of technological change: robots and AI. The first three step functions, or industrial revolutions, mechanization, electrification, and computerization, all had a profound impact on the organization of business and society.

Those changes, however, mostly impacted the industrial process: how we make things. New technologies allowed companies to make things more efficiently, increasing productivity and output. Simplistically, the increase in production and output allowed for cheaper goods which allowed for more people to buy those goods, which meant more goods were needed. This led to an increase in workers, as even with more efficient workers, more stuff was needed. This led to increased standards of living (we had more and better stuff) and more jobs.

In massively increasing productivity in how we make things, these industrial revolutions played no small part in transitioning most developed economics into service and knowledge economies. Services now represent nearly 80 percent of the US economic output and employment. With the next step function of change mostly impacting the service industries, the right name for this change is not the fourth industrial revolution, but rather the First Services Revolution. Will the changes coming to service employment be as dramatic as they were to manufacturing employment? Will the disruption be all the greater due to the size of the services economy? These questions drive doom in the hearts of workers and policy makers. But are they any different than the questions asked at the dawn of the last three technological step functions?

They all started with prediction of the coming doom of humankind as fewer and fewer workers would be needed. From the cotton gin and the weaving loom, to the assembly line and the personal computer, jobs were supposed to evaporate, workers were predicted to rise up, and society was expected to crumble. These past doomsayers are dismissed today as wildly pessimistic. Even Aristotle mused in his famous work *Politics* that if machines could sufficiently advance there would be no more need for human labor.

However, those predictions were not entirely wrong. Each change did lead to tremendous social upheaval and, in some cases, armed uprisings. While better standards of living were achieved eventually, there were painful transition periods, particularly for the communities that were displaced. A rising standard of living for all is hardly solace when the factory that closes is in your town.

Skynet: the fictional AI system that led to the rise of the machines and the war to terminate humanity in the movie The Terminator.

Rosie Jetson: the delightful and ever-helpful robot maid of the futuristic Jetson family in the animated children's TV show, The Jetsons.

We have a battle brewing for mindshare in the coming robot age. On one side, we have the Skynet Scenario, with titanic estimates of jobs lost and tales of doom, mimicking past doomsayers. On the other, we have those arguing the Rosie Jetson Scenario, with rising standards of living, an abundance of material things, and more leisure time as the robots do our mundane tasks for us. In between the two, we need to analyze what is different about this change from past ages of technological advancement. We will explore all these and offer a glimpse of what I believe the First Services Revolution will hold.

But let's start with some background on our subject, the robots.

Robots first came to the factory floor in the mid-1970s. The first versions were mechanical arms that could weld, paint, and lift objects. Their adoption was slow at first, as with any new technology. However, as the return on investment became apparent, we saw more widespread adoption starting in the 1980s.

According to the World Robotics Association (WRA), today there are about 2.1 million industrial robots in factories around the world. This number has grown between 10 and 15 percent per year over the last decade. This compares to a total robot population of approximately 17 million… the vast majority of which are vacuum cleaners from Roomba.

Industries with repetitive high-scale processes, like automotive and electronics manufacturers, dominate the usage of industrial robots. We will hear these words a lot in our exploration of how robots will impact the future of work via "repetitive high-scale processes," but more on that later.

> The decline in manufacturing employment in the US has led many to the conclusion that US manufacturing jobs were moved to factories in Mexico, China, or another low-cost economy.
>
> However, Ball State University did a study in 2015 that concluded that 88 percent of job losses were due to productivity growth as a result of automation and 12 percent was due to offshoring.

There is conflicting data on how many jobs have been eliminated by this first wave of industrial automation, which started during the age of computerization, or the third industrial revolution. In the US we have seen manufacturing employment decline from a peak of over twenty million jobs in 1980 to around twelve million jobs today. While manufacturing employment declined by 40 percent, manufacturing output has more than doubled. The fact of the matter is we produce more manufactured goods than ever before as a country; we just do so with fewer workers.

As we look to the future of robots, several forces are driving us toward an inflection point in robotic adoption. The price of the hardware and software that make up the robots is continuing to fall. At the same time the performance of robots is improving, making the cost-benefit analysis favorable to smaller and smaller companies, for more and more processes, and in more and more industries. Advances in sensors, gripping systems, balance, and AI allow for ever more applications for robots, including in the home. These factors combine with the increasingly networked nature of the machines (the Internet of Things), allowing for continued robotic learning and updating.

It is worth mentioning that while costs may be declining, and robotic capabilities and connectivity are increasing, robots are still massively expensive, clumsy, and dumb. A world where costs have fallen, and capabilities have increased, so that we can all have a Rosie Jetson in our homes, is still decades away. It will come, but not until well into the future.

Again, the largest challenge of the coming age of the robots is the application to the services industry. With the ability of software to perform increasingly complex and nuanced tasks, powered by AI, we are faced with the prospect of repetitive high-scale processes in the service industry being replaced by robots. This revolution will be known as the First Services Revolution as jobs like data entry, accounting, legal, and other administrative functions could be eliminated. Will the 40 percent reduction in manufacturing employment be mirrored by a 40 percent reduction in service employment? Do jobs in services have repetitive high-scale processes as 100 percent of their functions, as it was in manufacturing? This has led many to predict the coming age of the machines, the end of jobs, and the Skynet Scenario.

The Skynet Scenario

"The Robots Will Take All of the Jobs." "Factories With No Humans." "AI Will Automate All Work." The headlines of today paint a scary, hopeless dystopian future. They are also usually just headlines with more nuanced arguments underneath. My favorite two headlines of recent years: "McKinsey Predicts 50 Percent of Jobs Lost" and "Oxford University Predicts 47

Percent of Jobs Lost." Two of the most respected institutions of thought, McKinsey and Oxford University, are predicting doom, so it must be true.

In a recent report, McKinsey did estimate that across approximately 50 percent of occupations, at least one-third of tasks could be automated, implying considerable changes for many workers. McKinsey also estimated that up to 30 percent of the hours worked globally were susceptible to automation, and that between four hundred and eight hundred million individuals around the world could be impacted by automation.

In 2013, a study by Oxford University conducted the first comprehensive analysis of the risk of automation. The authors looked at 702 detailed occupations and assessed the risk of each job's potential displacement by emerging technologies such as robotics and AI. The conclusion was that 47 percent of jobs were at risk. The study was quoted frequently, and often incorrectly, that 47 percent of jobs would be gone. The authors didn't conclude that these jobs would definitely disappear; they just ascribed to each of the 702 occupations the likelihood that the job would no longer be needed. The likelihood of a job disappearing was based on the amount of work in that job that involved repetitive high-volume tasks. It led to a lot of hand-wringing, especially since the 702 detailed occupational listings allowed everyone to look at their specific job function and freak out.

Both McKinsey and Oxford though were talking about robots' and AI's impacts on jobs. Their studies and predictions were focused not on jobs *lost* but rather on jobs *changed*. These reports focus on a factor we have discussed before: that jobs are made up of component tasks. Some of those tasks are repetitive in nature and occur at a high volume, thus are susceptible to automation. The same task, done over and over, is what the first robots in factories replaced, starting in the 1980s. Those jobs consisted of 100 percent of tasks that were repetitive and high-scale, so those jobs were lost...in the millions. That's what McKinsey, Oxford, and other studies have been analyzing: which jobs have a high percentage of their component tasks that are repetitive and high-scale. Those jobs will be impacted with either loss or change as robots or AI perform those tasks. Fifty or forty-seven percent of jobs *impacted* is not fifty or forty-seven percent of jobs *lost*. Some of those jobs will be lost, of course, but the vast majority will not. But the headline in our social media-driven news cycle is HALF OF JOBS WILL BE GONE.

Of course, that is not to say that there are not very real concerns about job loss. Job loss from automation has already happened and will continue. Some industries will be impacted disproportionally; let's look at two of those industries.

Today there are four million professional drivers in the US. What happens to these workers in a world of autonomous vehicles? Autonomous trucks can deliver goods from factories and ports. Autonomous taxis can pick up riders upon request from an app. Autonomous buses can drive their routes and pick up and drop off riders at designated bus stops. Sure, we may not be that close to this future (I would imagine twenty years at least—sorry, Mr. Musk!), but the debate on autonomous vehicles is a discussion of "when" not "if."

Today, there are nearly three million waiters and waitresses whose jobs are also at near-term risk. They serve their tables, providing customers a piece of paper that lists everything on the menu. They return to take down, on another piece of paper, what people would like to order. They then bring that piece of paper to a different person to prepare the meal. Diners could instead just select menu items from a tablet on their tables, which automatically notifies kitchen staff (including some robots) of the order—and a huge percentage of waitstaff could be out of a job.

> Robert Williams, a worker at the Ford Motor Company Flat Rock Plant, was the first person killed by a robot. He was crushed and killed instantly by a one-ton transfer machine on January 25, 1979.

These two examples illustrate how automation could potentially eliminate nearly seven million jobs, or nearly 4 percent of the US labor force. How does society cope with that shift? How do the families of those workers cope with that shift? How does this not further exacerbate income inequality? This is the doom of Skynet. We aren't dreading killer robots launching a war on humankind, but the slow usurping of humanity's role in the workplace.

The doom of the future of work is not only lost jobs but also the increase in the gaps in our society. Those with the lowest education levels and skills have lost the most in recent economic history, causing an increasing divide in many societies between cities and rural areas, between service workers and manufacturing workers, between those with college degrees and those without. These divisions could be exacerbated by the rise of the machines, with grave impacts for society.

While we may not face 50 percent job loss, even 5 percent is enough to massively impact communities and cause widespread turmoil and despair. Government safety nets will buckle as more people use long-term disability, welfare, and other programs. Voters may look for easy and incomplete answers in populism and nationalism.

In order to cope with change at this scale and the fear of the coming job losses, the Brookings Institute has put forward some policy strategies to help communities deal with these shifts. I include them here as this is the most comprehensive and well-researched look at near-term solutions I have read.

- ▶ **PROMOTE A CONSTANT LEARNING MINDSET.** This is a common theme we see throughout the discussion on the future of work: the need for constant learning, reskilling, and change. Specifically, Brookings advises to invest in reskilling incumbent workers, expand accelerated learning and certifications, make skill development more financially accessible, and align and expand traditional education to foster uniquely human qualities. A tall order for sure, but a necessary step in adapting the workforce and harnessing new technology.

- ▶ **FACILITATE A SMOOTHER ADJUSTMENT.** As a society, we have to look at how to ease the transition for displaced workers. Brookings proposes a Universal Adjustment Benefit to support displaced workers (maybe through extended and increased unemployment benefits) and subsidize the hiring of displaced workers so they can reskill on a new job.

- ▶ **REDUCE HARDSHIPS FOR WORKERS WHO ARE STRUGGLING.** Society can't wait for workers to be displaced but rather should support those in low-skilled jobs that are susceptible to automation. This will reduce financial volatility for workers and allow them to adapt and begin their own reskilling.

► **MITIGATE HARSH LOCAL IMPACT.** Some communities are more at risk than others. If we allow certain regions to fall behind, we risk creating permanent tiers in society. Support should be focused on communities at risk, beyond easing the adjustment of workers themselves.

There is change coming, and that change will require society to adjust. Whether the change will be at the scale predicted by some or the policy suggestions by the Brookings Institute will prove to be fruitful, no one will know for years. Jobs lost. Families and entire communities displaced. Crumbling social safety nets. This is the doom of the Skynet Scenario and it cannot be dismissed. We know that much has already changed. We know more change is coming; we just don't know exactly what and where. What we do know is that this change will happen in a different way than previous technological step functions.

It's Different This Time

Before we look at the Rosie Jetson Scenario, let's investigate what may be different about this step function. The speed, global nature, productivity improvements, and impact on services all make this change that workers, companies, and society face different than the past.

The last three changes took nearly one hundred years to fully propagate through the economy. Due to the compression of the technological adoption curve and the increased connectivity of devices, the First Services Revolution may occur in as soon as twenty years. The technological adoption curve looks at how quickly society adopts a new technology. The telephone took nearly sixty years to get its first fifty million users. The mobile phone took fourteen years to reach that same milestone. Facebook took only three years. Pokémon Go took nineteen days. In addition, the Internet of Things means many devices are connected to each other and to the web. Thus, they can be sent software updates instantly, around the globe. Improvements to

Apple's AI assistant Siri that can now manage more of your life is only one iOS update from hitting 1.5 billion people.

Other differences may be the global nature of the change and the increases in productivity we see in this step function. The last three technological step functions happened locally and then made their way around the globe. There was time for localization. Due to globalization and compressed technology adoption curves, this change will happen in many places at once. Robotic process automation (RPA) software is being deployed as we speak in Berlin, Shanghai, Chicago, Sao Paulo, Mumbai, and Cape Town. This is not the textile mills in Cromford being improved and then slowly localized for Lowell, Massachusetts. This will happen everywhere at the same time.

Another difference is the potential for the productivity improvements with robots and AI to be much higher than the changes we have seen in the past. We won't know the answer to this difference for a while but given the productivity of advanced robotics and RPA software, we may find increases in productivity, and thus job losses, at a scale we have not seen before. RPA software can perform, without sleep, rest, or sick days, every data entry task a company needs to perform. This isn't Chad in accounting being able to process more invoices in a day, thereby allowing the elimination of two of the forty roles in accounting. This is the entire department being eliminated because software can perform all their tasks. Again, we have to wait to see how companies adopt these innovations, but the potential for disruption on a scale we have never seen does exist.

Lastly, I will highlight again how this change will impact the service economy in ways the other changes did not. That is not to say that services were not impacted in the first three industrial revolutions or that manufacturing will not be impacted by this change; it's simply to note that AI software and increasingly cheaper robots (with increased capabilities) allow for replacement of repetitive high-scale process in almost every industry. Given the size of the service economy, the brunt of the impacts will be felt in the service economy producing the First Services Revolution.

Services were not as impacted previously as services work is more difficult to standardize than an industrial process. Without standardization it's difficult to get the repetitive high-scale processes necessary for automation.

A factory line benefits from the same task being performed a billion times the same way; a call center does not. Well it could, but it wouldn't leave you with many happy customers. AI's ability to crunch massive amounts of data, however, changes the ability of a company to standardize, measure, and improve processes in a service economy.

Whether it's the transcription and analysis of every customer service call, with real time feedback to the operator, or the capturing of every bit of data on a customer and product, such that institutional knowledge now lies with the institution and not with any one worker, workers are at risk of becoming interchangeable. That word should strike fear in the hearts of every worker in the service economy as it did a hundred years ago for the manufacturing worker.

"Interchangeable" creates that fear because it exacerbates the supply and demand imbalance. Before a worker is interchangeable, there is a special skill or training needed for that function so the supply of workers with that skill/training help determine the supply and demand balance. If a worker becomes interchangeable then any worker can take their place. That means there is a drastic increase in supply with no necessary increase in demand. With an increase to supply the power in the relationship tilts massively to the creator of demand: the company. Creating interchangeability by standardizing processes in services is powering the feelings of dread about the First Services Revolution.

The Skynet Scenario may be faster, more global, and more impactful than any change we have ever seen.

The Rosie Jetson Scenario

At its heart the Rosie Jetson Scenario is an argument that the First Services Revolution will play out as each of the industrial revolutions has played out. There will be some dislocation for some workers, some adjustment for society, but in the end it will be massively beneficial in ways we can't even comprehend today. There will be new industries, new means of production, more leisure time, more goods and services, and a better future. Someone once said, the five most dangerous words in business are "this time it is different," as it is never different. So, the First Services Revolution is something to embrace and know that much like the first three industrial revolutions, we will all soon be much better off.

In the near future, robots and AI could provide all the goods and services we need at only a small fraction of the human effort that we use today. By performing the repetitive high-scale processes of work and at home, there could be a dramatic reduction in the number of hours needed for work. With that reduction we see a continuation of the historic trend of decreases in working hours discussed earlier in the book. The flip side of productive increases is that we can also expect that the cost of producing everything will drop significantly. With massive decreases in the cost of production, the cost of goods may also decline. These two factors combine to create a world where people won't need to work as many hours to be able to afford an ever-increasing standard of living.

These were the benefits of the last three industrial revolutions: the proliferation of cheaper goods and services at a scale never seen before and the creation of new things we had not yet imagined. The capacity freed up by companies and individuals has in the past unleashed creativity and innovation that has pushed forward the possible.

Robots will cook for us. Robots will clean for us. AI assistants will manage our schedules and make our appointments. Self-driving cars will manage our transportation needs. We need simply to order some cotton (grown in a robot-managed field as far as the eye can see), wait for the drone to deliver it to our doorstep, put the material into a 3-D printing machine, and a new shirt is ready for us in minutes, costing us less than a dollar. Oh, what a wonderful world!

People will have ample time and resources to focus on their interests and passions, like science, art, family, and leisure. There could be unprecedented abundance with a social infrastructure that ensures all individuals benefit.

We will work less, have enough income from that work (or from the state), and let our robot butler do most of the work while we paint and spend time with loved ones. Doesn't sound so bad at all.

We can look to the brilliant team at the World Economic Forum (WEF) for the best near-term analysis I have seen. In its *The Future of Jobs Report 2018*, the WEF team discussed how technological advances rapidly shift the balance between the tasks performed by humans and those that could be performed by machines. They predict that if these changes are managed wisely, they may lead to a bright future of good jobs, and improved standard of living for all.

The report goes on to estimate the near-term use cases of robots from 2018–2022 in various aspects of industry and society. From humanoid robots in the home (very limited) to non-humanoid land, underwater, and aerial robots (some applications in specific industries like oil and gas) to stationary robots (continued penetration at existing growth rates of 10–15 percent per year) to machine learning and artificial intelligence (currently attracting significant business investment and expansion).

In its survey of global companies, the WEF found that nearly 50 percent of companies expect that automation will lead to some job losses. The survey also noted that 38 percent of employers expect to increase their workforce in existing areas and 25 percent expect to have new jobs created by emerging technologies. This led the WEF report to conclude that by 2022 nearly 75 million jobs will be lost but 133 million jobs will be created—a net increase of 58 million jobs worldwide.

The job losses were focused on areas of repetitive high-scale processes such as data entry, accounting, assembly work, cashiering, driving, and legal. The job creation was focused on new roles such as data analysts, information security, software development, robotics specialists, and digital transformation workers. Job growth was also focused on the expansion of productivity in existing roles in sales and marketing, social media, e-commerce, engineering, and human resources.

The WEF report also provides a sobering look at the challenges we face as a society, with a focus on the need for reskilling, constant learning, and training (similar to the Brookings Institute policy recommendations). It begins painting a picture of a future of abundance, although it doesn't offer hope for a Rosie Jetson in every living room in the next five years.

The Reality

The reality is change will come but not nearly as quickly as many fear and not in all industries that many fear. Technological advances will unfortunately put many people out of work. But we can trust that, with the realities of the Labor Equation and the lack of regulatory reform, change will come slowly to the labor market. While the technological adoption curve has compressed, that doesn't mean that the technological advances will be on the road and in our homes soon.

Changes of the scale of the First Services Revolution require the regulatory framework in each industry to catch up. Change of this type is incredibly complex and costly, and companies will move slowly before adopting technologies that displace jobs in mass. For something like autonomous vehicles, while the cars may be fully road ready in five years, the legal and regulatory frameworks on liability and licensing, let alone the charging infrastructure and road sensors needed for mass adoption, will take much, much longer. In addition, the complexity of the situation means the changes that everyone thinks are coming are usually not the changes that are coming.

A very informative example can be found with the automated teller machine, or ATM. The ATM first made its appearance, according to Chemical Bank, at its branch in Rockville Centre, New York, on September 2, 1969. When the ATM achieved mass adoption in the 1990s, many predicted the death of bank teller employment. Why would anyone need a teller when a machine is there to dispense cash and take deposits? Those predictions proved massively wrong as the number of bank tellers in the US increased alongside the proliferation of the ATM. According to the Bureau of Labor Statistics, the number of teller jobs increased from about 500,000 at the beginning of the ATM proliferation to about 600,000 today.

This has led to a common refrain that the future of work can be seen in how bank tellers upskilled with ATMs powering the quality of work and producing job growth. As ATMs took over mundane tasks, tellers were retrained as customer service representatives able to cross-sell products such as mortgages and investments. Thus, the machines are good and will make our lives better and create jobs! This is an interesting albeit incomplete analysis.

The ATM-teller relationship reflects the future of work in as much as it has complexities to it that belie a simple job creation or job destruction story based on technology. Teller jobs did increase but mostly due to banking deregulation, allowing banks to race across the country opening branches. One of the reasons they were able to open so many branches is that it was cheaper to operate a branch because, with the ATMs, each branch required fewer tellers. Some estimate the average bank branch went from having twenty-one tellers to thirteen tellers due to the ATM. As the branch turf war between banks ends (I am pretty sure there is one on every corner in Manhattan now), mobile apps allow for more remote banking, and ATMs increase in capabilities, this story is far from over.

Tellers may now be out from behind the glass with an iPad to service all your banking needs, but will there be another 20 percent increase in employment over the next twenty years? Seems highly unlikely. A 20 percent reduction as more tasks are automated? Possibly. But again, it's a complex issue, as are all issues incorporating labor and technology.

If we look at the Oxford, McKinsey, WEF, and other studies on the future of work (and I have read them all) to see which roles have a high degree of repetitive high-scale processes, we start to get a picture of which jobs really will be eliminated. Again, jobs where the vast majority of the tasks in that job are repetitive high-scale process are the ones that will face high percentages of elimination. Even in a world where robots and tablets can perform all the tasks of a waiter, there will still be waiters, just not as many as are employed today. People will always want, and pay for, the higher level of service and personal touch a human brings.

The research tells me that jobs lost will be at about 10–15 percent of all existing jobs. Those jobs will be in functions such as assembly, transportation, food preparation, bookkeeping, payroll clerks, other accounting functions, cashiers, legal services, and data entry. Another 5–10 percent of jobs will be created in either new fields like robotics and data science or in fields requiring human or creative interactions such as design, sales, marketing, operations management, organizational development, IT services, information security, ecommerce, social media, culture and people specialists, digital marketing, and innovation. I am also adding in another 5 percent of job increases in fields we have not thought of yet.

Thus, I am predicting *no net change* in the number of jobs in the United States over the long term.

This will be coupled with a continued decrease in the number of hours worked, as the largest impact will not be jobs lost or jobs created but how almost all jobs will change. Nearly all jobs will change as mundane tasks are done by software and robots. This will lead to a decrease of about 20 percent of hours worked across all industries, quite possibly in the form of a four-day work week.

This result is due to the fact that only 5 percent of jobs have 70-100 percent of their tasks that are repetitive high volume. These jobs will be eliminated over time.

Another 25 percent of jobs have 50-70 percent of their tasks automatable. This will lead to some jobs lost as jobs are consolidated (if four people have the same jobs where 50 percent of tasks can be done by a machine, it's likely that only two have jobs at some point). Other jobs in this group will be repurposed to new functions or see a reduction in working hours. This is what gives us the other 10 percent of jobs lost.

As for the other 70 percent of jobs where the repetitive high-scale tasks represent less than 50 percent of their function, these jobs will simply change and have a slight reduction in hours. Not many jobs will be lost from this group and it's this group that drives the bulk of the future of work.

Jobs lost, jobs gained, and jobs changed.

As for other predictions, here is what my research tells me about the world of work in 2040:

► The labor force participation rate remains stable at 63 percent for the next twenty years as two trends offset each other: the baby boomers retiring and extended healthy working life leading to delayed retirement.

► Due to people working longer and increased immigration, the total size of the labor force increases from 164 million today to 176 million; the US is the only industrialized country to increase the size of its labor force.

► Union membership will reverse its decline and reach 20 percent but through entirely new union structures that are loose associations across companies, organized digitally.

► The federal minimum wage will be $20 per hour as the online worker movement is successful in pushing local and then federal changes.

► The percent of people with a four-year college degree peaks at 35 percent in 2020, declining to 30 percent as technical schools provide more skills-based education.

► Worker-retraining programs are standard at all companies and are done with VR technology as the changing nature of work means continuous learning is a requirement for all workers.

► There have been no sweeping regulatory changes: no third employment classification, no Universal Basic Income, no huge changes (but rather incremental ones) to the way we tax capital, labor, or wealth, because these changes are driven by economic crises and we will avoid a crisis over the next twenty years.

► The on-demand labor market peaks at 40 percent of the labor force in 2034 and remains constant at that level for generations as technology continues to bend the labor equation to the maximum process that can be done by on-demand labor.

Overall the prediction is that we have a much more balanced society, where the cost of production has fallen, allowing almost every member of society to massively benefit from higher standards of living. We will be ever closer to a society free from want and that is immeasurably good. However, the transition to this wonderful place will not be easy.

We face this next revolution at a time when our counterbalancing forces are especially weak. Unions are at their lowest level as a percent of the labor force in over one hundred years. Regulations are being rolled back at the federal level, and the social safety net is under tremendous financial pressure due to an aging population. All this is occurring while government debt levels are at historic, and some would say unsustainable, levels, and we have the most unequal society in recent history.

Not a great place to start this transition. But it's not really the start. The age of robots and AI has already begun. The power balance has already started to shift, although somewhat mitigated by the tight labor market. Robots have already displaced nearly 40 percent of workers in manufacturing. Robotic process automation software is just the new name enterprise software companies have been using to streamline processes and eliminate jobs for years. Jobs lost to robots and AI is not something new at all.

And the counterbalancing forces are beginning their rise. Union membership may be low, but union sentiment is at its highest levels. The "Fight for 15" movement is an example of how a modern union can amplify its power in the digital age, rallying public support. Regulations may be rolling back at the federal level, but states are stepping into the breach with waves of regulations designed to protect workers. Sadly, the social safety net doesn't have an upside hope. Government coffers are stretched, public pensions are massively underfunded, and as the baby boomers retire there are no easy answers to getting to solvency, let alone an expansion.

History has shown the need for these counterbalancing forces. While my prediction of no net job loss with a 20 percent decline in the number of working hours may seem optimistic, the transition of jobs alone is enough to cause large-scale disruption. We will need to be conscious of those left behind; individual, families, and communities displaced. A relatively small loss of the total jobs in the economy is no solace to a community where a factory or mine closes. The counterbalancing forces in society must be ready to support those left behind.

Most importantly we must retrain workers in a more efficient way. The 15 percent of the labor force that will lose jobs must be helped to transition to the fields where jobs are being created. This will be one of the largest challenges for our society as we usher in the First Services Revolution. Retrain, retrain, retrain. It can't just be up to the workers; society must put in place the polices to encourage workers and companies to focus on continuous learning.

The reality is we, as a society, get to help determine how this will play out. It's up to us what kind of education system we want, what kind of tax policy we want, what kinds of social safety nets we want, and what kind of worker protections we want. The reality is there is a brilliant future waiting for us, but immense challenges for those at greatest risk of displacement, and thus all of society, in the near term.

I believe we will navigate this change and eventually arrive at a Rosie Jetson–like future, where society is free from want. However, while I won't pretend that the transition will be easy, I remain hopeful in what the future of work holds for everyone.

CHAPTER 10

PREDICTING THE WORLD OF WORK IN 2040

"The only thing to do with good advice is to pass it on."

—Oscar Wilde

THE TASK OF STUDYING THE PAST AND ANALYZING THE PRESENT IN order to make predictions about the future is behind us. In front of us lies the most exciting part of this journey. During my nearly ten years running WorkMarket (the last two as a part of ADP), I have had the pleasure of meeting many great thinkers on the world of work. These include industry leaders, policy makers, advocates, professors, executives, and union leaders.

I am humbled that twenty of the most interesting, thoughtful, and smartest thinkers have agreed to share their thoughts on the future of work. These are the people shaping the future of work. What follows is not edited for content; each writer has produced their own work. They are writing in their format of choice (no one chose haiku, despite my encouragement) about the world of work in the United States in the year 2040. Their focus was entirely up to them, and I could not be more grateful for their contributions to this book.

As an added incentive, our twenty writers are competing for the Future of Work Prize. I am personally putting up $10 million as the award for whichever writer in this book is the most correct when the clock hits January 1, 2040.

The writers in alphabetic order by first name are:

Andrew Stern	President Emeritus	Service Employees International Union
Barry Asin	President	Staffing Industry Analysts
Bruce Morton	Head of Strategy	Allegis Global Solutions
Carl Camden	Former CEO	Kelly Services
Cindy Olson	Former CHRO	Enron
Daniel Pianko	Managing Partner	Achieve Partners
David Fano	CEO	Teal
Deborah Borg	CHRO	Bunge
Gene Holtzman	Founder	Talent Tech Labs
Gene Zaino	Founder	MBO Partners
Holly Paul	CHRO	FTI Consulting
Ian Ziskin	Former CHRO	Northrop Grumman
Jane Oates	President	WorkingNation
Johnny C. Taylor, Jr.	President	Society for Human Resource Management
Kim Seymour	CHRO	WW (formerly Weight Watchers)
Marcus Sawyerr	CEO	Yoss
Michael Bertolino	Senior Partner	E&Y
Michael Johnson	Former CHRO	UPS
Michelle Greenstreet	Former CHRO	Various
William Weissman	Partner	Littler Mendelson

So here are their thoughts in their own words:

Andrew Stern *is the president emeritus of the Service Employees International Union, which grew nearly one million members under his leadership. SEIU was the country's largest grassroots political organization and a leader in the efforts to pass Obamacare and in the Fight for $15 minimum wage. He is the author of two books on jobs and the future of work and is a proponent of a universal basic income.*

January 1, 2040

Dear Family:

Having spent the majority of my life trying to improve the lives of people that work and their families, I wanted to try to offer my thinking about the world I believe you will experience as we celebrate New Year's this 2040.

The future will provide us all the necessary technological tools to create a world with enormous opportunity to promote more individual choice, prosperity, sustainability, equality, longevity, and security.

Artificial intelligence, data, robotics, the internet, 5G, automation and technological achievements from autonomous vehicles to personal robotic assistants, constant health monitoring and preventative treatment will make us safer, allow us to live longer, while requiring less time for the responsibilities of daily living.

And yes, we now are fully aware that the smug economists and "expert who assured workers that the idea of a tsunami of technological job l was mere hysteria, and that the economy in this transition will again cr more jobs than it destroys in occupations of which we could not even dreamed, have been discredited. They bear much of the responsibili our failure to plan for these radical changes in work and jobs, and th we are still trying to dig ourselves out of.

You now find a world where three-quarters of the early twe century nongovernmental jobs, except those in the low-paid "cari omy, have disappeared, as both muscle work and mind work disp ple from the highest-skilled white-collar jobs to the largest o categories of retail, truck driving, healthcare administration, and delivery.

Capitalism and the private sector failed America miserably in the area of job creation. Despite all the CEOs' calls for reskilling and retraining, corporations pocketed their profits as labor costs declined and shifted responsibility and blame to the government and an underfunded public education system, neither of which had the ability, track record, or in reality, as business knew, any real ability to create massive numbers of private-sector jobs.

You experienced how, during the last decade, 2020–30, inequality continued to increase, the richest 1 percent continued to receive most of the economic gains, and neither Democrats nor Republicans were able to harness the growing and widespread unhappiness into any kind of programs to radically transform our economy.

But in 2032's presidential election, people voted for a new populist party and for fundamental change. First, the newly elected Democratic president was forced to act by the pressure created from the massive electoral gains of the new "Equality Party" that campaigned on a series of simple, but bold, economic proposals. The first of which was introduced by the president and congressional leaders immediately in both houses of Congress. It laid out a roadmap for the government to redistribute wealth through a universal "American Dividend" of $25,000 for each citizen and required children under twenty-one perform national service to be eligible for their dividend going forward.

Second, Congress passed new parameters for health care, capping the total US expenditures at 15 percent of GDP by 2038, while ensuring that no individual would pay more than $1,000 in premiums, co-pays, or deductibles. Policy experts predicted, and it is now true, that this framework would radically transform the American healthcare system to one be based on promoting health, not disease management, and value, not procedures.

Third, the government created universal childcare and elder care vouchers, which allowed the proliferation of a variety of pathways for people to choose care for themselves or their families at a level of payment enough for both living wages for caregivers and offering new noninstitutional choices.

Fourth, the government passed legislation to establish lifelong education accounts, which allowed people to pursue new skills, training,

apprenticeships, higher education, and for the first time, courses emphasizing spiritual learning or self-enrichment or personal self-improvement.

All these new national initiatives were financially possible as a result of the establishment of "The American National Trust" created first by transferring all the existing public and private contributions for health care, in addition to government welfare, child and elder care programs, into the "The Trust," which acted as a sovereign wealth fund. Second, for the purpose of creating enough new resources to meet these programmatic initiatives, it was supplemented by a combination of revenue-raising policies that included VAT, asset/wealth, estate, data, carbon, and financial transaction taxes.

As a result of this robust raising of the economic floor, securely financed for the long term for every American, the issue for you and your family to confront in 2040 is neither your economic well-being nor whether the world can make enormous progress in areas such as medicine, food, lifestyle, or carbon reduction. More significantly for you and all society, the question to be answered is whether humanity can, for the first time, climb toward the highest level of Maslow's needs hierarchy—achieving one's full potential, self-actualization. And there are obstacles.

Although the country has made massive positive strides through technological advances and wealth creation and distribution, issues of greed, racism, tribalism, government authority, and surveillance will need to be addressed in order to secure your family's future. Simultaneously, the world will face the challenge of whether countries can collaborate to solve international crises, such as climate change and migration, or whether these issues and others will only increase policy and resource conflicts.

You are at a tipping point, an inflection moment, where questions of economic well-being are replaced with profound questions of the meaning and purpose of life. A world where global cooperation and human interactions can push us toward fulfillment and peace that I could not have even imagined or, instead, toward a dystopia with the worst tendencies of humanity, bred by scarcity and extreme inequality, led by corrupt governments with unlimited power to suppress and monitor our every thought and action.

This is the world of 2040, and you are on the front lines of writing the next chapter of humanity.

As one who spent my life working for justice, peace, and happiness, I hope I can count on you to continue to lead in that direction. Because if not us, then who? And if not now, then when?

I love you all!

Sincerely,
Andy

A leading authority on workforce solutions worldwide, **Barry Asin** *is renowned for his expertise on staffing and contingent labor. President of Staffing Industry Analysts (SIA) since 2010, Asin holds overall responsibility for the company's strategy, operations, and growth on a global basis. Asin is the coauthor of Breaking Through: Leadership Disciplines from Top Performing Staffing Firms and is a frequent speaker at industry events, sharing essential insights on leadership and the challenges, opportunities, and rapid transformations around work today.*

Where Are We Going?
The World of Work in 2040

If we want to look to the future of work in 2040, more than twenty years away at this writing, it's useful to think about the sorts of changes that we've seen in work over the *last* twenty years. While some things are radically different between 2020 and the year 2000, others have changed only slightly or not at all. And that, of course, is the question at hand. Which trends will continue at their current rate, which will accelerate rapidly, and what sudden surprises does the future have in store for us?

Where We've Been

So, what have we seen over the last twenty years in terms of the world of work?

As I'm most closely involved at SIA in researching and studying the world of contingent work, staffing, and the gig economy, I've paid close attention over the past twenty years to how that ecosystem has evolved. Temporary staffing annual sales have grown significantly to now exceed $150 billion in revenue in the US. Meanwhile, we have seen even faster growth in contingent work overall. Our latest study concludes that Americans spent $1.3 trillion (yes, trillion with a *T!*) on contingent/gig work in 2018. It also finds some fifty-three million Americans doing contingent/gig work at some point in 2018, nearly 37 percent of the US workforce. This includes the full range of agency temporary workers, internal seasonal/

temporary workers, independent contractors, statement of work consultants, and human cloud workers engaged in work via online platforms.

This growth has happened in part because it has increasingly suited both employers and workers in a world now decidedly beyond the old model of lifetime employment. Additionally, much of the growth in contingent/gig work has come about due to the dramatic and ongoing march of technology, with the big story being the impact of the internet on the world of work. During the 1990s, job boards were a huge improvement in speed and cost over the old job advertising model via newspaper classifieds. While that impact had been dramatic, by 2000, most of the practices for engaging and managing talent had changed very little, with the change that existed coming via automating—but not fundamentally changing—existing processes.

Since 2000, tech-driven change has continued unabated, and we've seen technology develop that has made it easier and easier to connect workers and hiring managers, and increasingly to provide all the services around that work that was once done in a manual or ad-hoc fashion. This has been exemplified in the world of contingent work by the growth of cloud-based Vendor Management Systems (VMS) to consolidate and track the often hundreds or even thousands of staffing vendors providing workers at large enterprise companies. While in 2006, some 16 percent of large companies had a VMS in place according to SIA's survey of buyers, today over 80 percent of large companies have a VMS in place. The growth of VMS technology led to a wave of services around it, including outsourced management of contingent workforce programs as delivered by Managed Service Providers (MSPs), the growth of Contingent Workforce Management as a profession, and the creation of a whole new and often quite complex talent supply chain for enterprise companies. While this happened in the contingent labor space, similar tech-driven innovation in technology to track and manage traditional workers has also progressed.

Today we can see that the increasing power of internet tools and the speed of systems is allowing online platforms to go beyond what VMS technology did and let workers and hiring managers connect and do work with very little human intervention in between, something we describe as the "human cloud." As with most technology adoption and change, the gating factor is not the capabilities of the technology and the tools, but the ability of people and organizations to understand how to use the new technology to their best advantage, and how to build organizations, incentives, and processes to leverage the new tech-enabled capabilities. Perhaps most importantly, change moves slowly due to the natural human and organizational resistance to it, particularly in large and successful organizations.

In addition to technological change, the past twenty years have seen an ongoing aging of the US population, lower birthrates, and a decline in growth of the labor force and labor force participation as the mass entry of women into the workforce has worked through the system. This slower labor force growth has helped exacerbate an ongoing gap between the skills needed by employers and the skills of available workers. Witness the BLS Job Opportunities and Labor Turnover Survey (JOLTS) data, which now shows a gap each month of approximately 1.5 million more job openings than hires, a situation never before seen in this data series.

Future Work

Looking forward, what might these trends imply for the world of work in 2040?

Let's start with a relative softball: demographics, one of the most precise forms of forecasting. After all, it's relatively easy to know how many eighty-five-year-olds there will be in twenty years, since they are all alive and sixty-five years of age today!

For better or worse, the short answer is that our future looks very much like Florida today.

Why is that? Assuming moderate changes in mortality and birth as well as similar immigration rates (suddenly not so certain in the age of Trump), the US Census Bureau projects that by the year 2040, 21.6 percent of the population will be over sixty-five, up from 15.2 percent in 2016. For comparison, Florida in 2010 had 17.3 percent of its population over sixty-five. Additionally, for the US as a whole, those over eighty-five will be the fastest-growing segment of the population, projected to equal 3.9 percent of all Americans by 2040, up from 2.0 percent in 2016. In 2010, only 2.3 percent of Floridians were over eighty-five. And the aging trend is already much more significant elsewhere in the world, particularly in Europe and Japan.

Given the low savings rates of the average American and the likely coming crisis in Social Security and Medicare (suggesting lower benefits and higher costs), odds are that many in this over-sixty-five group are not going to be able to fully retire. Many of them will also not have the interest, the health, or the stamina to work in a traditional full-time job, making them ideal candidates for new and more flexible forms of work. Today, SIA surveys show that older workers are among the ones most receptive to temporary labor.

Combine an aging workforce with an ongoing skills gap, and I see the world of 2040 as one where talent, particularly highly skilled talent, is increasingly in the driver's seat in the ongoing push and pull between workers and employers. By 2040 the fears of the late teens and early twenties that robots and AI will take our jobs will have morphed into the reality of previous technology innovation. Yes, there will have been disruption and locally painful changes in jobs, but overall, AI and robotics will become tools that enable new jobs, take previously repetitive and low-value-added tasks away from workers, and allow humans to do the work that humans do best, including creativity, person-to-person interaction, persuasion, and a variety of other soft skills not easily automated. In fact, given our ongoing and increasing talent gap and shortage of workers, AI and robotics will be more needed than ever to enable economic growth in a time of labor scarcity. This is already playing out in Japan, one of the oldest societies on the planet and a society with a heavy use of robots and other tech gadgets to automate work.

How will all those empowered workers engage with employers in the year 2040?

Due to the extreme worker shortage, by 2040 I believe that most companies will increasingly find ways to get the talent that they need when, where, and how the workers want to be engaged. In terms of *when* that means workers will work on flexible schedules wherever possible based on their own personal choice of when to work and when not to work. All that will be scheduled through AI-driven tools that make finding and doing work as simple as Amazon is making it to buy products today.

Meanwhile, with the full embrace of the digital age, 5G technology, and mobile computing, the answer to where work will get done will more often be remotely, potentially anywhere in the country or the world. This implies office space designed only for the important but less frequent face-to-face meeting days, or perhaps even that coworking spaces will fully mature and continue developing into social centers where like-minded or like-skilled people independently work together by choice.

Finally, workers will be engaged in the manner they most prefer. While our surveys confirm that most workers want the stability of a traditional job, many do not. Driven by the need for flexibility and control, one in five Americans prefer a contingent or other flexible form of work. With the aging population, this will only increase by 2040. That means significant growth in all forms of contingent work.

All this will happen in a much more fluid way that we are only now beginning to see the outlines of among the most progressive and leading-edge organizations. Today we refer to the practices of many of these leading-edge organizations as Total Talent Acquisition (TTA) and Total Talent Management (TTM). Essentially these terms describe the idea of organizations proactively managing their full range of talent options when it comes to getting work done. The reflexive response historically was that whenever there was a job that needed doing, the answer was to hire a full-time traditional employee; by 2040 the standard procedure and organizations will include considering the full range of talent options to execute the work. This means robots and automation first, then the full range of contingent and outsourced options second, with traditional employees reserved for those roles deemed strategic, long-term, and core to the organization. HR will lead these efforts, assisted by artificial intelligence that will factor in all the elements of cost, quality, speed, and risk management to best determine how roles, departments, or entire business units should utilize different categories of workers.

In a future world of ongoing talent shortages, we will also see a dramatic change in the role of education in preparing the workforce of the future. By 2040 a significant percentage of traditional colleges and universities will have failed due to financial pressures on their outdated economic model. In their place, we will see more and more company-driven skills-based training delivered in a flexible and often remote boot camp–style model. These models exist today in companies like Revature and Talent Path, where twelve-week technology boot camp skills training is paired with a staffing-firm model placing graduates into companies with acute talent shortages. Trainees don't pay for the educational classes, but instead commit to work at client companies for a period of time in exchange for forgiveness of the cost of the training. By 2040 these models will have evolved to embrace a wide variety of different skills, and a majority of workers will get their skills training from these hybrid educational/employer-based training models.

Additionally, as it does today, the legal and regulatory system of 2040 will continue to have an outsized impact on the development of work. Today we see significant strains in traditional legal definitions of employment that were designed for the old factory/industrial era. This is most seen in the controversy over the misclassification of employees as independent contractors. By 2040 most nations around the world will have established new categories of workers, somewhere between an independent contractor and an employee in terms of status. These "dependent contractors" will have explicit guidelines for their treatment by employers in terms of pay, benefits, working conditions, and more. Additionally, in the US we will finally see a decoupling of employment from the healthcare system, which will ignite an explosion in interest of alternative forms of working once traditional jobs are no longer the primary way to ensure healthcare needs are covered.

Finally, I'd like to close with a little bit of humility. Although twenty years into the future seems far away, no doubt there will be many things about the year 2040 that will closely resemble the world today. Some things, though, will be completely surprising from today's perspective. Work, like the rest of the world, can be profoundly influenced by "black swan"–style unexpected events that catalyze major societal change. On the positive side, it's likely that some new technological breakthrough that we can scarcely imagine today will have a significant impact on the way people in 2040 work. We can already easily imagine changes in the world of AI and robotics as well as advances in biotech and other areas of science that may completely upend our current notions of work (and humanity for that matter).

Meanwhile, the potential for highly disruptive negative changes in society on the political front is suddenly readily apparent, with the possibility of renewed conflict between nation-states and peoples that could prove as disruptive as previous world wars. Or perhaps by 2040 we face the possibility of dire changes from out-of-control climate change, as it turns out that climate scientists have been overly conservative in their predictions in the face of political backlash. Both of these scenarios suggest major population relocations, a situation that may fit well with the trend toward remote work, particularly for professional jobs. However this larger future evolves, what once was rarely imagined could go from not at all on the horizon to an imminent reality. As it has in the past, work will be shaped by the larger society, for better or worse.

Bruce Morton *is in his fortieth year in the human capital industry and is well known as a global workforce design and talent acquisition expert. In his current role, Bruce serves as Global Head of Strategy for Allegis Global Solutions. He has designed, implemented, and managed some of the largest talent resourcing solutions across many different parts of the globe and has been recognized as HR Thought Leader of the Year by HRO both in EMEA and in the US, and he recently published a book, Redesigning the Way Work Works.*

Welcome to 2040. It's amazing to think that just a short twenty years ago the role of Work Design Architect didn't exist!

But How Did We Get Here?

These people who understand, design, and give strategic advice on the best way to get work done in all those mega-successful companies you read about really are today's corporate heroes.

Work Design Architect

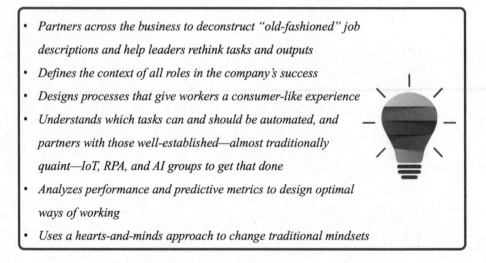

- *Partners across the business to deconstruct "old-fashioned" job descriptions and help leaders rethink tasks and outputs*
- *Defines the context of all roles in the company's success*
- *Designs processes that give workers a consumer-like experience*
- *Understands which tasks can and should be automated, and partners with those well-established—almost traditionally quaint—IoT, RPA, and AI groups to get that done*
- *Analyzes performance and predictive metrics to design optimal ways of working*
- *Uses a hearts-and-minds approach to change traditional mindsets*

So, how are they achieving their success?

The role obviously requires the ability to deeply comprehend an organization's business objectives and translate those goals into a structured workforce architecture and framework. Here we take a deeper dive into how that translation has played out.

Obvious synergies exist between this role and that of a design architect in the construction industry. For physical structures, design architects analyze sites and create plans for construction, remodeling, additions, and/or repairs. They attend to the style of the finished project while meeting all building requirements and codes. An even better construction analogy is that of quantity surveyors. They take the blueprint drawing of a house and calculate which resources and materials are needed to build the structure, as well as lay out the order in which everything should be built. They create a critical path analysis and time frame for each stage of a project, plus a cost/time/quality-versus-risk profile. A **work design architect** does exactly that by taking the business objectives as the blueprint and designing the best way to get the work done!

Breaking Organizational Barriers

Have you ever watched the studio credits roll after an animated feature film? There's the director, the assistant director, the effects designer, storyboard supervisor, texture artists, shaders, and animators. Then there are people who do lighting and fixing, and someone called the render wrangler (what the heck is a render wrangler?). And don't forget the caterers! The credits go on forever, listing multiple people in myriad roles. Did you ever think all those people were employees of the studio?

So, organizations finally woke up and caught up with the movie business, in which hundreds of people come together, make a piece of art, and move on to the next project. Some companies have, of course, maintained a nucleus of employees who are routinely augmented on an as-needed basis with contingent workers. This overall structural shift was the crucial driver of agility; that is, in essence, what has allowed us to optimize the work that our people now do. Within that agile state lies the prime source of business leverage: the ability to get more out of that key person than a competitor would. How? By the way the organization is set up.

When companies truly understood the value of deconstructing the work, the light bulb went on. That was the moment we started answering these seemingly simple questions....

What are we truly trying to achieve as an organization? What is our core business objective? Describe what our business will look like in two years if we have totally hit the ball out of the park.... How are we getting work done? With which type of people? What kind of contracts do we offer them? How can we invest the required time to truly understand what each of the functions inside our company is working toward, individually and as a whole?

What are we truly trying to achieve as an organization? What is our core business objective? Describe what our business will look like in two years if we have totally hit the ball out of the park.... How are we getting work done? With which type of people? What kind of contracts do we offer them? How can we invest the required time to truly understand what each of the functions inside our company is working toward, individually and as a whole?

Yes, we knocked it down to the roots. We finally asked, why are we here? What are our dreams? What do we want to be when we grow up?

Most companies now use data visualization tools to create talent architecture depictions of how work is getting done. My favorites are the wall-sized 3-D holograms that show your workforce, color- and shape-coded by geography, type of worker, volume, tenure, cost, and so on. I love to see the vision hologram of what you believe this needs to look like in two years to achieve your business objectives. And of course, the fun starts when we tune our Amazon glasses to VR mode and have the "How do we get from hologram A to hologram B?" conversation!

The successful company leaders stopped working *in* the business and worked *on* the business. They asked the CFO where the company should be in one or two years, then they asked the CPO, the CEO, the CTO—not about a vague wish or something off the vision or mission statement, but what it was going to take to get where they want to be. *What do they want their function to be known for in the next one or two years? What is their branding? Their messaging? What talent do they have on hand? What kind of talent are they going to need to get to that point?*

One of the interesting things that came out of that process was the realization that Human Resources teams could be guilty of being the cobbler's children with holes in their shoes—not really comprehending the above or their function.

But how did companies clear their headspaces to think about things differently?

You guessed it, I am zeroing in on the entrenched divisions that stood in the way of building the ideal talent base, organizational design, and hiring platform: HR and Procurement. The two departments were, by design, at odds. Human resources types saw investment in labor paying off by managing people properly to get the best performance. Procurement gurus believed returns were tied to speed, efficiency, and cost management, which could be achieved through work design or through stringent job requirements. The reality and awakening came when we finally got to a combination of these things in the late 2020s, when C-level Workforce Transformation departments were created, driven by the company's goals and outcomes of the actual work completed, and produced the ROI.

That end to the old ideological split that was causing a natural breakdown in communication between the two sides, as they vied for control—the bad old days—had gone! Finally, the people on both sides of that virtual wall started asking: *Do we have the right talent architecture to achieve our objectives? How do we get to that point?*

Yes, this was a huge undertaking for the more established organizations—and we saw start-ups gain competitive advantage for a while as they were far more agile—but well worth it in relation to the massive size of the prize that was achieved. Organizational readiness literally spurred a quantum leap in the economy and a new advantage over the competition for the talent those companies needed.

Let's take a quick walk down memory lane and look at some of the ways those organizations got started:

► **They evaluated and updated past models for matching workers to work.**

Traditionally, employers were filling open positions with the same type of worker who just walked out the door. That meant automatically putting full-time employees or temporary contractors in the same slots. Sometimes it took someone outside the organization to drill down and ask the tough questions about what the work actually needs, and which workers are available to vie for the job.

► **They mapped the performance of current talent/work matches.**

Analyze those segmented job summaries. The goal of this evaluation was to understand how efficient and effective hiring decisions were and to see where improvements could be made to better match the work to workers. This was particularly important when considering which tasks could be automated.

► **They defined how each job role was meeting overall business goals.**

This required a cross-departmental conversation, with the outcome directed at HR and Procurement. Linking positions or assignments to larger objectives revealed how individual actions come together to achieve them. This also showed which job skills produce which results. With that information, those who were doing the hiring could seek competencies, rather than rely on academic degrees and x number of years of experience.

► **They streamlined and automated work processes.**

By now, companies had surveyed or had informal talks with their employees about how work works—and where it doesn't work quite so well. They relied on them to suggest which tasks are redundant, less efficient, or a pain in the neck. They then huddled with project leaders and managers to redefine workflows and truly automate those robotic tasks that were being carried out by humans!

This was a win-win effort for everyone. They continually reshaped their work methods toward improvement, and at the same time, made work easier or more enjoyable for employees.

Try telling your kids how we used to get work done and they'll look at you as if you are mad—some things never change….

Carl Camden *received his doctorate in Communication from Ohio State University in 1980. In the intervening years he was a tenured professor at Cleveland State University, President of Wyse Advertising, and CEO of Kelly Services. He is currently co-founder of iPSE-U.S., advocating for the rights of Independent Workers.*

Written with: **Hollie Heikkinen** *is an expert advisor to national associations and companies. She serves as Trustee and Co-Chair of Advancing Women in Corporate Leadership for the Committee for Economic Development (CED). She is also a leading member of the Coalition for Workforce Innovation (CWI). As Founder and CEO of iWorker Innovations, Hollie brings decades of experience to the fight for the rights, fair access, and equality of Independent Workers.*

Secretary of Labor Annual National Independent Worker Day Speech
August 16, 2040

As Secretary of Labor, I would like to welcome you all and thank you for being here today as we celebrate the twenty-first annual National Independent Worker Day.

Steve Jobs once said, "Your work is going to fill a large part of your life, and the only way to be truly satisfied is to do what you believe is great work. And the only way to do great work is to love what you do. If you haven't found it yet, keep looking. Don't settle. As with all matters of the heart, you'll know when you find it."

I believe that as a nation, we have found *it*. We have found the freedom to work the way we want without putting our families or businesses at risk. But let us not forget the history of the US labor force. When ten thousand carpenters, machinists, and craftsmen took to the streets of New York during 1882's inaugural Labor Day parade, there was plenty to protest: the US workforce consisted of twenty-five million people—including children as young as ten—working seventy-hour weeks in unsafe environments, and they were still not earning a living wage.

Fast-forward to 2020 and you were more likely to see crowds gathering at a department store sale than marching on behalf of labor protections. Some might say that we took for granted the hard-won rights that unions secured over a century of struggle; child labor laws, safe working conditions, forty-hour work weeks, and a minimum wage all became ingrained into US social norms. Unemployment had reached historic lows. "Good jobs" delivered access to a suite of government-sanctioned rights. Employer-sponsored benefit packages protected workers and their families.

But we were fooling ourselves as we sat satisfied with that progress.

Motivated by the ideals of freedom and entrepreneurship, America's Independent Workers—consultants, freelancers, "1099s," the self-employed—bravely forged careers outside the carefully drawn boundaries of government and corporate protections. They weren't eligible for workers' compensation if they were injured while working. They didn't receive disability pay when they fell ill. They didn't have access to employer-funded health coverage or employer-managed retirement savings. They lacked parental leave programs and anti-harassment protections.

These Independent Workers were parents caring for young children; children caring for elderly parents; millennials on the move; boomers not ready to retire; Gen Xers and Yers who broke free from corporate constraints and took their skills directly to the market. As a group, they were more highly skilled and better educated than the traditional workforce. Ranging from accountants to coders to crafters and every profession in between, America's Independent Workers were contributing a staggering and annual $1.4 trillion to the US economy. Yet they were denied the protections granted to full-time employees simply because they worked a different workstyle.

And, so, in 2020 the rally cry became:

> *It's time for Labor Day—and labor policies—to reflect the new reality of work.* It's time to once again gather and rally the voices of millions who work unprotected. It's time to remove bias and barriers and build a better way forward for America's workers— one that includes ALL the people whose daily contributions are shaping our country's future. It's time to put meaningful reform

behind the US Department of Labor's rhetoric: *"It is appropriate that the nation pays tribute on Labor Day to the creator of so much of the nation's strength, freedom, and leadership—the American worker."*

Yet, over sixty-eight million Americans still worked without a safety net. We did begin to see change as opinion leaders, politicians, educators, and the media, enlightened by Jeff Wald's book, *The End of Jobs*, recognized a revolution in the world of work was well underway. Hashtags seeded the memes of the rising workstyle. A leading staffing agency coined hashtags like #whatsnext and #ditchthescript. Meanwhile, iPSE-U.S.—America's only association dedicated to giving Independent Workers an equal voice in public policy, an equal choice to pursue their workstyle without fear, and equal access to business solutions and benefits—propagated hashtags like #lovethewaysyouwork and #officechoice. The hashtags became the banners of the rise in political and economic power, recognition, and hope of New Labor.

Today, we celebrate the end of the "job dystopia." Citizens, young and old, organize work around their lives, rather than being told by management how to arrange their lives around a job; this, because after the seventy-year job experiment in America, an unspoken rebellion against the job dystopia ensued, and nearly seventy million Americans decided to work as Independent Workers. We called them by many names then, including gig workers, freelancers, independent professionals, digital nomads, and ultimately Independent Workers. We are grateful for those people who led the way and helped secure the paths that led us here today. Your freedom to love the way you work was secured by a movement of people who decided that they did not have to be mindless job drones. They chose to make their work fit their lives, and not make their life fit their work. And today, iPSE-U.S. is the largest association of labor in the United States.

As a nation, we no longer celebrate "Labor Day," though we don't discredit those who carved out paths before us. And many of the remaining craft and trade unions are allies or share membership with iPSE-U.S. Today on this twenty-first annual National Independent Worker Day—we celebrate you!

We can all smirk a little bit as we look at one another, real humans, real people who continue to live their lives the way we want, celebrating our professions. You were not replaced by automatons, artificial intelligence, or hive intelligence as it was once said you would be. You represent over two-thirds of this great nation's workforce. You empower the US and, increasingly, the global economy. You have led the way in innovation and technology and are nothing less than unstoppable.

Please take a minute to congratulate yourself and the enormous amount of talent that sits in this room. Thomas Jefferson said, "I find that the harder I work, the more luck I seem to have," but today we proudly say, "The smarter I work, the more luck I seem to have." You have worked smarter; you continue to advance in your profession by completing certificates and relevant training.

Gone are the days where we completed one-and-done bachelor's degrees and sold our services to the highest bidder in a process that we called the job search. We no longer search for jobs, rather we choose from a broad array of opportunities that are presented to us. We haven't been replaced by robots. Instead, technological and educational advancements have given us more options to work the ways we want. We rely on immersive experience technology, continuous self-directed education and certification, and so on to keep us competitive and satisfied in the workplace as talent satisfaction metrics replace antiquated employee-satisfaction scores.

You have contributed to the US economy, and now we can proudly say that we have successfully implemented Universal Basic Income for All. As Ubies, we have equalized access to resources and opportunity by providing every citizen with basic income. It provides the support needed for Independent Workers to update skills and increase their market competitiveness without relying on antiquated "jobs" training.

As our communities of Independent Workers continued to develop and the exodus from corporate buildings took place, we did look back. We are conscious and mindful of our impact in the world. We looked back with a collective conscience to leave things better than we found them. We have successfully converted the behemoths that used to be corporate workspaces into practical and affordable living spaces. We have recognized our role in the changed educational landscape, and we worked diligently to ensure that university campuses that were once filled with "degree-seeking" students are now small specialized epicenters for continuous learning and training.

We took on the challenge of fighting unintentional bias and discrimination by deinstitutionalizing medical benefits, other insurance products, and income continuation and retirement products, and *we won*! We have remodeled the tax collection systems that were once relegated to employment-collected-based services to a tax collection process that is portable because *our work comes to us*.

In conclusion, many of us grew up scared of a world of unremarkable sameness. Instead, we now work and live in an amazing multiverse that celebrates our uniqueness. We celebrate a world limited only by our imagination and willingness to risk occasional failure.

I am proud to say that even if you failed along the way, as Independent Workers you failed forward, and you have succeeded. Once again, thank you, and happy twenty-first annual National Independent Worker Day!

Cindy Olson, *who currently leads The Choice Executive Strategic Alliance, is an Enterprise Executive Level Leader who, while CHRO at Enron, built the first truly integrated Human Capital Management system with SAP. As part of Enron's twenty-person executive team, she played a critical role in leading Enron to be the first company named Fortune's Most Innovative six years in a row and the twenty-second-best company to work for.*

The Future of Talent Acquisition and Utilization in the Year 2040

In 2000, Enron was the seventh largest of the Fortune 500 companies. The company, by that year, had become the first to be named as Fortune's Most Innovative six years running. The relatively new Enron Broadband business unit was in the process of formalizing a partnership with Blockbuster to bring movies on demand to consumers, and we were talking about the "Cloud" in our Vision documents. That year, Broadband livestreamed Shania Twain's halftime performance at the Super Bowl on computers all over the world.

I was then the EVP of Human Resources and Community Relations for Enron and a member of the twenty-person Executive Committee. Our HR Team was working with McKinsey and the IT organization to build the first integrated HCM on our SAP platform, and it was being built to include employee profiles, much like the LinkedIn of today, and employee self-service. At that time nothing existed like that in the marketplace, so we had formed a small team to figure out how to monetize the investment we had just made in this innovative technology. The result was a joint venture with Accenture to white label that Human Resources–managed services offering and sell it to other organizations including Goldman Sachs and American Express.

At the time, we knew we were about fifteen years ahead of the market, and when I jumped back into the HR world in 2015, it became clear that we had built something that was, even in 2015, ahead of its time. Today, as I look at how fast technology is changing our world and how the iPhone's invention has changed everything in our consumer life, I can't help but think about how all that will surely change how people work. Where they work and what devices they use and what they expect from the technology they use to do their everyday jobs will grow more and more important as a differentiator of where talent will want to work.

Many organizations are not going to be able to keep up with those expectations, resulting in them *not* being able to either attract or retain great talent for their business. Unfortunately, because I was at Enron for twenty-three years, I will not be able to hold an executive position in another company; however, it is because of that extraordinary experience that I have been trained to be curious about what the future could look like. How an organization attracts, utilizes, and retains their talent is changing rapidly.

By the year 2040, you will see rapidly changing requirements from the workforce of the future that will impact every organization in three major areas.

1) Defining who your workforce consists of and how you attract each segment will be very different.
2) What the "jobs" will look like in the organization will change considerably.
3) The technology requirements of the workforce will be the key to attracting and retaining talent.

Defining Who Your Workforce Consists of and How You Attract Each Segment Will Be Very Different from Today

There are all kinds of statistics that indicate the workforce of the future must be thought of as a combination of full-time and part-time employees, contractors, freelancers, and retirees (from their own organization and also from organizations that have not figured this out). The workforce options are generally agreed on by most consulting firms, but it is the percentages of each where differences of opinion exist.

In the energy sector, there is an average of 35 percent of the larger organization's employees who will be retiree eligible over the next five years. The work they do will continue to be needed, so utilizing employees as contractors or freelancers through a "labor cloud" makes a lot of sense. By 2040, many (I will go out on a limb here and say 60 percent) organizations will be utilizing their retirees in this fashion. The baby boomer generation is not ready to retire and go play golf.... Some want to stay relevant, others want a purpose, and there are those who do need the money.

In addition to working on projects or assignments, I believe that retirees will also be utilized as "interns" who train either employees or freelancers because of the institutional knowledge they hold.

An increasing percentage of the workforce will require flexible schedules and will prefer "gigs" at several companies to mitigate their risk of working for one employer that is not able to provide diversity of assignments or have the loyalty to their workers. Therefore, I believe that trend will result in even college recruits coming into the organization as freelancers. They will also prefer this status because of the frequency of pay, immediate feedback, and ability to provide pay equity, which will become more important to attract younger talent.

My prediction, therefore, is that the workforce distribution by the year 2040 could look like this:

Freelancer/Contractors	80 percent
Full-Time Employees	20 percent
(this includes college recruits/retirees)	

What the "Jobs" Will Look Like within the Organization as They Evolve into "Assignments"

With the prediction that freelancers and contractors will make up a majority of the workforce, the structure of what we consider "jobs" today will transform. Teams with specific assignments will prevail, and AI will be at a point that you will know the makeup of the most productive teams and be able to mobilize and replicate those teams easily depending on the assignment.

For example, the "job" of an accountant, which consists of several objectives monthly like booking revenue, balancing the books, and creating balance sheets and income statements, will be split up into assignments, and workers with the appropriate skills will be assigned those tasks based on those skills and past performance.

In the energy industry today, the retiree-eligible workers hold "Jobs" that do maintenance in the field. Things like compressor station maintenance and repair may be split into compressor station maintenance on a set schedule and the repair would be assigned to the closest worker who is available to do that assignment.

The transportation industry could benefit from using this concept right now, as there is a huge driver shortage nationwide and self-driving trucks may not be ready in twenty years because of the risk. Drivers, however, could be assigned to take the loads from a hub to the final delivery point with a driverless car on the interstates driving from point A to point B.

I can see marketing roles split into assignments, including roles that would be focused on the different kinds of website content. Other assignments could include social media placements or campaign development. I have heard of marketing interns being hired into an organization, and they are not being asked to take on more difficult assignments. The work they are given is described by them as "grunt work." To enhance their résumé and be able to learn more, they may be working for another company as a freelancer on the side, because that company is willing to challenge them with more difficult assignments.

In a survey that we had the employees of Enron participate in only four months prior to filing for bankruptcy, we learned something that was unbelievable. I was horrified at the response to the question "Are you currently using all your skills in your job?" Only 35 percent said they were. Think of the capacity we were leaving on the table and, more importantly, the job satisfaction or employee engagement that was suffering as well. I could not believe that even though employees were working an incredible number of hours, they did not feel they were utilizing all their skills. If you look at this statistic for today's organizations and workforces, it is still about the same across the board. Only about 35 percent of the workers believe they are using all their skills at work.

I believe there are employees in your companies today who would love to take on a project that stretched them beyond what you think they are capable of doing by giving them increased experience that helps make them more valuable in the marketplace. I have always felt like it is the organization's job to hire the best, develop them so everyone in the world wants them…and then keep them!

After reconnecting with many ex-Enron employees, I have heard the same thing over and over…they would not be where they are today without being allowed to step up and do more than they ever thought they could. I believe in the year 2040, the successful organizations will allow even their employees to take on additional assignments to build their skills.

The Technology Requirements of the Organization's Talent Will Continue to Evolve as the Technology Used in Our Consumer Lives Evolves

Today a large percentage of households in the world utilize a "Siri" or an "Alexa," yet very few organizations offer that level of and ease-of-use technology options today. This is already becoming a glaring problem for companies saddled with clunking legacy systems that are not able to be changed easily.

Even in the year 2000, Enron launched voice-activated search and dialing for our telephony. It was not as accurate as it is today, but we could ask the phone system to dial another employee and it would do that.

The Gen Z future workforce currently experiences, from a very young age, their parents' devices that keep them engaged, stimulated, and occupied constantly. As they enter the workforce over the next few years, they will not be satisfied with using technology to do their assignments or jobs that does not give them that same experience.

Over the next twenty years human resources executives *must* drive this new worker experience, which will be a critical requirement to attract and retain the talent needed to drive business results. The "jobs" must be restructured into assignments and labor clouds or talent communities formed to be able to handle the assignments that result. Human resources will be required to work in tandem with the organization's IT leader to make this happen. It will take an immense amount of confidence and courage to do this, but without that kind of transformational leader, the organization's business will suffer from a lack of the best talent possible.

Daniel Pianko *is co-founder of Achieve Partners and prior to Achieve was co-founder of University Ventures, one of the largest investors in education companies and technology. Achieve is pioneering the employer pay models described in this chapter.*

Staffing company CEOs think their competition is other staffing companies. But revenue growth is stalled not by a dominating competitor or hard-to-replicate technology but because of a lack of talent. In six of the last twelve months, the number of open requisitions is up but the total number of staffed positions is down because there aren't enough trained workers to fill hard-to-staff positions from software engineers to nurses.

The source of the problem is simple: staffing company executives and sales people focus their talent sourcing efforts (LinkedIn, Indeed, or other) for a limited subset of relatively publicly available sources for specific talent. Sourcing talent is a question of identifying the limited number of people with the same skill set. Specific nursing credentials or programming languages are like gold.

Gold, however, can be mined. More gold can be found and sold. Staffing companies have historically relied on universities and corporate America to build and develop skilled individuals. But talent creation—really skills creation—is perversely stalled. There are only 20,000 computer scientists graduated each year—and that number is relatively stable over the past twenty years. The number of nursing school graduates has approximately doubled over the same time period—but still left a million-worker shortage in licensed healthcare professions. Even lower level skills are in high demand, with a lower labor participation rate driven by people who have opted out of employment.

Universities have not just failed to produce the required talent, but learning at universities is notoriously disassociated from the work force. According to our research, while 96 percent of provosts think that their university is preparing graduates for the world of work, only 14 percent of hiring managers think that college graduates are prepared for the world of work. The result is that 43 percent of college graduates find a first job that does not require a degree. The problem is even worse for those looking to reskill—if college didn't work the first time, why would college work for someone who has been out of the workforce for some time?

The world of work has also changed. Applicant tracking systems and online job boards mean that every job listing now results in hundreds or thousands of applicants. Sorting through too many résumés means that hiring managers are adding a dizzying array of technical skills to job descriptions. At the same time cost of a bad hire means that employers are basically limiting hiring to people who have "done" the job before. Perversely the increase in specific certifications and skills is driven by the explosion of job applications to job board listings, which means fewer applicants filling the "spec" required in an expensive-to-fire world. The result is massive hiring friction.

While employers are becoming more demanding and universities are effectively running in place, it's no wonder that the world of staffing companies feels squeezed. Talent knows their worth, and companies are looking to constantly reduce expenses. Ever-shrinking margins and slowing growth seem to be the topic of every Staffing Industry Association meeting. Staffing companies have merged into a smaller number of behemoths who have some pricing power.

But size wedded to a traditional staffing model is not the answer. To remain competitive in the twentieth-first century, staffing companies will have to become increasingly integrated talent developers and providers. They will have to mine for gold, not just distribute it. Adecco has led the way by acquiring coding bootcamp leader General Assembly for $400 million in 2018. Investcorp, the private equity firm, recently acquired Revature for over $200 million. Innovative staffing companies are starting to think about how to grow the funnel of talent rather than just find the right person for a specific opportunity.

What does the new model look like? Staffing companies transform from merely identifying talent and placing the resources to creating custom training programs for employers. End clients will alert a staffing company that they will need 100 resources with a specific skill set—say a dev ops environment or a type of nurse. Then the staffing company will provide training classes to sufficient students to fill that demand.

The new model will require major changes from the entire value chain. The most immediate impact is that staffing companies will have to dramatically expand their capital base. Under the new model, staffing companies will have to source, train, and take placement risk before getting revenue from a resource. In the above example, a staffing company might have to source 150 cognitively capable individuals, run them through a dev ops training course, pay those trainees while non-billable, and then assume some "leakage" before placing the cohort of 100. Then payment will be stretched out over a one- to two-year contract.

More capital will not be enough. Staffing companies will become differentiated on brand and training offered. Staffing companies will try to source strong cognitive functioning individuals who don't have the skills that employers are seeking. Sourcing talent will shift from LinkedIn to a college campus—or the unemployment office. Suddenly screening becomes critical: how do you distinguish between an out-of-work engineer capable of (or excited about?) being retrained vs. someone who is burned out and can't (or won't) become current on the latest technology. Once in a training cohort, the ability to predict skills that will be in high demand and teach them effectively will become the key value proposition.

Perhaps the biggest shift is the relationship with the end client—the employers. Employers today have a list of approved staffing companies and, when a position becomes available, send out a rec and whoever fills the rec fastest gets paid. In a future state, sales people will create a strategic relationship with employers about their talent needs six, twelve, even eighteen months out. Employers will make long-term "buy" decisions from their preferred partners at premium rates. But the premium pricing will not come cheap—employers will look for the staffing company to take the risk on sourcing, training, and "fit" with the employer.

To account for this change, staffing companies will have longer relationships with their employees that frequently stretch multiple years as a resource develops from junior to senior. The financial relationship may also change—with novel financing tools for education, like employer-paid Income Share Agreements becoming the norm to ensure that resources pay for the training they receive. Temp to perm becomes the norm—but it's more like temp to permanent partner to the employer and the employee.

In an age where entry-level hiring is broken, and mid-career restarts are few and far between, staffing companies become more like the talent development and sourcing arm of large corporates rather than a job shop. Strategic sales people will work closely with HR managers to identify long-term talent needs and then agree to fill rates. Getting a job at a top staffing agency will be sought after, creating a real differentiated value proposition.

General Assembly, the Adecco unit, calls this new model "Talent as a Service" (TaaS). While TaaS may not become as highly valued as Software as a Service ("SaaS"), the new model does drive a much higher return on investment. The new models frequently have gross and net margins two to three times typical staffing company margins.

So, in 2040 when every staffing company realizes they are really in the education and skills-development business, what does the landscape look like? The changes will likely be quite revolutionary. Clayton Christianson famously predicted that half of all colleges would close by the mid-2020s—while his timing was off by a decade (or more), we are already seeing increased closures and mergers of higher education institutions. Many colleges and universities will not adapt to the changes that are reshaping the economy. Basic education is too expensive (student debt exceeds $1.5 trillion in the US) and not closely tied to return on that investment.

But don't count out colleges and universities: many will dramatically lower their prices and start to integrate more with the employment ecosystem. Selective institutions like Harvard will act much as they have for over a millennia: select the future leaders of society. But the vast majority of schools (over 95 percent) are nonselective, and students seeking higher education will increasingly turn to mega colleges, like Arizona State University and Western Governors University, whose dominance of the mass post-secondary market will only grow.

While the colleges and universities evolve, staffing companies will change perhaps more drastically. The term *staffing company* will likely disappear. Instead, staffing companies will become branded entry level (or mid-career repositioning) opportunities. Successful staffing companies will develop brands that feel a lot more like "Accenture" than "Kelly Services." These new brands will identify high-performing talent, provide skill development, and certify skills to end employers. Staffing companies will feel much more like consulting firms than job shops.

Staffing companies have had the same business model for thirty-plus years: find clients, get orders, develop a list of talent, and connect the two. When does the staffing company CEO realize she's managing a copper line telephone company a few years after the introduction of cell phones?

David Fano *is a serial entrepreneur and senior leader known for building high growth teams. Most recently he served as Chief Growth Officer of WeWork, where he was responsible for driving their rapid expansion and as a result increasing revenue 100 percent year over year for four consecutive years to a $4 billion annual run rate.*

Written with: **Erik Martin** *is a marketing and community expert who has led high growth teams at Nike, reddit, Depop, Airtime, and WeWork. He's been named one of the world's one hundred most influential people by Time Magazine and a top fifty innovator by Adweek.*

In 2016 the National Center for Chronic Disease Prevention and Health Promotion (NCCDPHP) released a report stating work-related stress is the leading workplace health problem and a major occupational health risk, ranking above physical inactivity and obesity.[1] Whether it's an increase in work hours, a volatile work environment, or a lack of interest in the actual work, people are experiencing job burnout at an increasing rate.[2]

Today, employers and employees are treating work-related stress and other workplace health issues with therapy, medication, and coaching. Though this is a positive step, too often these treatments only address the symptoms and not the underlying problems. An increasing body of research shows that, on average, meaningfulness of work is more important to individual employees than any other aspect including pay, opportunities for promotions, and working conditions. When a person finds meaning and purpose in their work, it can provide fulfillment and a positive buffer

1   National Center for Chronic Disease Prevention and Health Promotion, "Workplace Health Promotion: How CDC Supports a Healthy, Competitive Workforce," March 12, 2019, https://www.cdc.gov/chronicdisease/resources/publications/aag/workplace-health.htm?mod=article_inline.

2   Zoë van Dijk, "From Moms to Medical Doctors Burnout Is Everywhere These Days," *Washington Post*, March 29, 2019, https://www.washingtonpost.com/national/health-science/from-moms-to-medical-doctors-burnout-is-everywhere-these-days/2019/03/29/1cea7d92-401d-11e9-922c-64d6b7840b82_story.html.

against undue stress. While increased connectivity and speed could make modern life more stressful, advances in technology possess a greater potential for workers to find their own meaning in the workplace of 2040.

Several factors can lead to increased meaning in workers' lives in 2040. The first is personalized algorithmic agents that have the ability to take on tedious "meaningless" tasks. The second is an increased ability for individuals to see how their work has impacted their lives; to find links between their current and past work; and to see how their current work could lead to their future plans. The third factor is an increased alliance between— and leverage created by—dynamic communities of individual workers who share personal causes, values, and desires.

Meaningfulness is closely correlated with happiness, but they are not identical.[3] A classic example of how they can diverge is parenthood. Parents often state that raising children is the most meaningful experience of their lives, yet in the moment that experience is not always considered a happy one. People often describe a similar paradox when reflecting upon meaningful work, but that does not mean it translates as a particularly happy experience in their career.

The future of work will not necessarily be one where everyone has a sense of purpose and connection at work, but an increasing number of people will have more freedom and more tools to focus on what brings them meaning. The individual worker, not the company, will drive this meaningful work, and the path will be different for each individual depending on their personal situation. Recent research has shown that meaningfulness not only is "intensely personal and individual" but is also episodic with "unplanned or unexpected moments" of deep meaning.[4] Nonetheless the workplace of 2040 will provide significant new opportunities to focus on meaningful work and address the deeper issues that contribute to workplace stress.

3   Scott Barry Kaufman, "The Difference between Happiness and Meaning in Life," *Scientific American*, January 30, 2016, https://blogs.scientificamerican.com/ beautiful-minds/the-differences-between-happiness-and-meaning-in-life/.

4   Catherine Bailey and Adrian Madden, "What Makes Work Meaningful—Or Meaningless," *MIT Sloan Management Review* (Summer 2016), https://sloanreview.mit.edu/article/what-makes-work-meaningful-or-meaningless/.

Meaning Created by Intelligent Agents

In almost all cases employers have greater resources than employees and greater reasons to gain efficiency. Therefore, employers invest in and primarily benefit from efficient technology. We have seen this unfold throughout history, be it with the advent of the printing press, machining process, robotics, and automation. It's only been when the employee possesses enterprise-level leverage that you see individuals investing in their own infrastructure. Historically, this has happened through collective associations like labor unions and in industries, like sports and entertainment, where employee talent has strong connections with large numbers of consumers.

People desire to be in the driver's seat of their careers. That is one reason we're seeing people switch jobs at rates higher than ever.[5] By 2040 the average worker will have more opportunities and granular choices to drive their own careers. Continued gains in computing power, connectivity, and accessibility will make the cost of technical infrastructure low enough that individuals will realize significant efficiency gains from minimal investments of their own time. They will have more and more powerful tools to share their thoughts, experiences, talents, and creative expression with a consequential audience. This will allow an increasing number of people to enjoy investments in infrastructure and media that were once only available to large enterprise and the elite.

This new infrastructure will probably take the form of intelligent agents. Powered by artificial intelligence and decades of data, these agents will fill our knowledge and skill voids. There will be no need for an architect to remember every building code because their personal "building code" agent will be ever-present while they design and can spring into action when the designer needs them. Assume the same will be true for doctors, lawyers, or accountants. The value of what we today see as experts will be in their ability to be creative and original, and not recite history from memory.

---

5   Robert Half, "Does Job Hopping Help or Hurt Your Career?" press release, April 5, 2018, http://rh-us.mediaroom.com/2018-04-05-Does-Job-Hopping-Help-Or-Hurt-Your-Career?utm_campaign=Press_Release&utm_medium=Link&utm_source=Press_Release.

We are even seeing the beginnings of this behavior in the customer service market where conversational chatbots can answer customer questions more efficiently than humans.[6] In the consumer market we take for granted the individual's ability to self-diagnose on WebMD, obtain legal documents on Nolo or LegalZoom, and get taxes done on TurboTax. Technology is positioning itself in a place where it can observe work and surface knowledge in real time. Imagine two more decades of increased advances in this area, and it becomes easy to envision how the individual will have access to relevant tribal know-how and the institutional knowledge that previously lived somewhere hidden in the enterprise.

Besides filling in knowledge and skills gaps these intelligence agents could address some data overload and time deficit problems that increasing connectivity has created. Your network of intelligent agents could filter and curate both the data the individual is generating and the data the individual is consuming. The individual worker of 2040, equipped with intelligent agents, will offload tasks they consider tedious and meaningless. The individual worker will possess the ability to not only fine-tune their consumption patterns of media but adjust their organizational communication to reduce time spent on information they consider meaningless. Future knowledge workers will have more control to seek meaningfulness in their day-to-day experience when they have the capabilities to invest time and personal desires in determining the tasks they want.

Meaning Created by Connections

Rapid advances in communication and organizational technology along with the rise of distributed teams and remote work have increased individual productivity. For the individual worker this productivity increase has often come at the cost of abstraction and disconnection. It has created an experience where knowledge workers are, in the words of philosopher Alain de Botton, "diluted in gigantic intangible collective projects, which leaves us wondering what we did last year and, more profoundly, where

---

6   Jon Walker, "Use Cases of AI for Customer Service—What's Working Now," Emerj, January 31, 2019, https://emerj.com/ai-sector-overviews/ai-for-customer-service-use-cases/.

we have gone and quite what we have amounted to." In *The Pleasures and Sorrows of Work*, de Botton suggests that the craftsperson does not suffer from this abstraction and disconnectedness of their work because they "can step back at the end of a day or lifetime and point to an object—whether a square of canvas, a chair or a clay jug—and see it as a stable repository of his skills and an accurate record of his years...." In twenty years, one can imagine that algorithms or personal automation agents could significantly help individual workers understand how their work contributes to larger collective projects. Like the craftsperson, the individual worker will be able to appreciate their work from a different perspective.

For example, an experiment run by author and Wharton Business School professor Adam Grant showed that when a university call center fundraising staff had a five-minute conversation with a student who had received a scholarship, the average number of calls made doubled and the weekly revenue went up 400 percent.[7] That connection to the positive impact on a specific individual turned abstract and exhausting fundraising calls into work that had more meaning.

In 2016, MIT conducted a study with 135 people working in ten very different occupations who shared stories about times they found their work particularly meaningful.[8] The work was often meaningful when it correlated with specific individuals they knew, such as family members. Knowing how one's work impacts real people is extremely motivating. However, workers often do not have access to the context or raw human feedback to appreciate how their work contributes to real-life outcomes. Intelligent mechanisms should be able to bypass organizational silos, anonymize personally identifiable information, and show how disparate tasks and functions connect across the organization.

Besides a connection to personal impact, there is another type of connection that research shows can help individuals. People find their work more meaningful when there's a connection to their own distinct story.

7   Adam M. Grant, "Leading with Meaning: Beneficiary Contact, Prosocial Impact, and the Performance Effects of Transformational Leadership," *Academy of Management Journal* 55:2 (2012): 458–476.

8   Bailey and Madden, "What Makes Work Meaningful," https://sloanreview.mit.edu/article/what-makes-work-meaningful-or-meaningless/.

Social psychologist Roy F. Baumeister found that while happiness relates directly to the here and now, meaning "seems to come from assembling past, present, and future into some kind of coherent story." Organizational systems and personal tools will track and index just about everything workers do in 2040. Though this massive data trail has troubling privacy implications, one positive possibility is that individuals will have an increased ability to look back. They can understand how their past actions and learnings connect with their present undertakings, and have the ability to project forward into their own probable but imagined futures with greater detail and fidelity.

In 2040 an individual worker could have some lifetime software companion that tracks their various experiences, projects, desires, learnings, successes, and failures. It will help surface connections for the individual to reflect upon throughout one's career. This intelligent career companion could augment a worker's ability to make meaning in the same way an excellent coach or advisor might today. This ongoing lifetime of learning is one where a knowledgeable advisor assists the individual by making suggestions, guiding, and coaxing self-reflection which could have a huge impact on people's lives. Though empirical studies on coaching are limited, there is evidence that it improves one's personal efficacy and motivation.[9]

We are already seeing these trends emerge as workers raised in a post-internet world express desires for greater overall connection to their work. As a 2017 report on the Future of Work by Deloitte stated, "Most Gen Z professionals [born in the 1990s to early 2000s] prefer a multidisciplinary and global focus to their work, with the expectation that this can create opportunities for mobility and a rich set of experiences." The report also stated that "Gen Z professionals, like Millennials before them, typically expect frequent coaching and feedback."[10]

9   Elouise Leonard-Cross, "Developmental Coaching: Business Benefit—Fact or Fad? An Evaluative Study to Explore the Impact of Coaching in the Workplace," *International Coaching Psychology Review* 5:1 (2010).

10   Carolyn O'Boyle, Josefin Atack, and Kelly Monahan, "Generation Z Enters the Workforce," *Deloitte Insights*, September 19, 2017, https://www2.deloitte.com/us/en/insights/focus/technology-and-the-future-of-work/generation-z-enters-workforce.html

If individuals can follow and connect on a personal level to the interdependencies within a department, company, business ecosystem, and even local communities, then individual workers will have more opportunities to bridge the gap between the abstract corporate and the relatable personal realm. This ability also prompts workers to connect with and reflect upon their own experiences and could help large parts of the 2040 workforce derive greater meaning from their own work.

Meaning Created by New Collectives

The relationship between worker and employer is long and complicated. At its most basic, you have a corporate entity intent on making a profit and a group of individuals enabling that aim. At its best, they align and bring about a mutual success. At its worst, employers exploit workers and take exclusive advantage of success and upsides.

Throughout history workers have organized to create an infrastructure that can fairly balance resources between workers and employers. Guilds, labor unions, and other institutions have helped provide the communication and coordination necessary for workers to take collective action and bargain for their fair share. Talent agencies have aided in the infrastructure where representation and advocacy were fundamental in providing that fair balance for the talent like those in the entertainment and sports industries. The talent agency concept dates back to a time when Hollywood was gaining commercial success and the actors, directors, and producers struggled against the power of the film studios. Groups of talent created entities like United Artists, formed by Charlie Chaplin and colleagues, that aimed to support talent through representation and advocacy.

Today, we see technology's potential to lower the cost of communication and coordination infrastructure to a point where workers can dynamically organize or create leverage without the aid of unions. They have the ability to maintain control of their career more than what they would with the backing of an elite talent agency. In 2019 knowledge workers at companies like Google, GitHub, and Activision have successfully organized walkouts and/or widely publicized communications to protest and demand changes when their employers' business decisions have not aligned with the employee values.

In the National Basketball Association, commentators frequently refer to the current moment as the "player empowerment era." The leverage the players have due to their direct connection with fans beyond the platforms controlled by the teams or the league is unmistakable. The players' influence and ability to build growing revenue streams outside of payment from their employers allow them to determine their own fate more so than previously. In a 2040 workplace setting, these same emerging tools that are only available for elite tech-savvy workers and star talent will be available for most workers.

The collective infrastructure that employees will have access to in 2040 can counterbalance the power of enterprises. Though enterprises will have access to tremendous tools and data, the collective intelligence of groups of employees backed by data, machine learning, and artificial intelligence will wield significant leverage. In the same way that talent agencies allowed creative artists in the entertainment industry to have more creative control than under the previous studio system, workers of 2040 could enjoy their own technological agencies. These dynamic collectives of individuals will coordinate, negotiate, and communicate their shared interests.

Ideally companies optimize for a unified intent or mission. Even when acting and communicating collectively, the workers do not have that singular intent. They can align around common causes and in mutual support, but each individual has a personal and unique set of outcomes they aim to solve. With improved communication tools, dynamic and perhaps temporary collections of workers may be able to wield collective power, while allowing for the varied desires and goals of the individuals.

Bringing It All Together

The nature of meaningfulness is fragile and highly individualized, yet research shows that making work more meaningful is one of the most powerful and underutilized ways to increase productivity, engagement, and performance. In one survey of 12,000 mostly knowledge workers, 50 percent said they did not get a feeling of meaning and significance from their work. Those who did reported they felt 1.7 times greater job satisfaction; they were 1.4 times more engaged; and they were over three times as likely to remain with their current employer.[11] Another study found that meaningful work could serve as a buffer against both depression and work stress.[12]

A business has operational departments for strategy, finance, people, branding, communication, and many others that support their success. In 2040, workers will have the same. They will have intelligent agents, connections to the history of their work, and connections to each other that will help them every step of the way. As neurologist and author Oliver Sacks says, living or working on a day-to-day basis is "insufficient for human beings; we need to transcend, transport, escape; we need meaning, understanding, and explanation; we need to see overall patterns in our lives." The worker of 2040 will have powerful tools to see the "overall patterns" in their projects, experience, and careers. In 2040 work will still be stressful and people will have to deal with new stressors that we cannot yet anticipate. But the worker will have more support to understand how that work connects with their purpose and have access to more tangible ways to find and pursue work that is meaningful to them.

11   Tony Schwartz and Christine Porath, "Why You Hate Work," *New York Times*, May 30, 2014, https://www.nytimes.com/2014/06/01/opinion/sunday/why-you-hate-work.html?_r=1.

12   B. A. Allan, R. P. Douglass, R. D. Duffy, and R. J. McCarty, "Meaningful Work as a Moderator of the Relation Between Work Stress and Meaning in Life," *Journal of Career Assessment* 24:3 (2016): 429–440.

Deborah Borg *is the Chief Human Resources and Communications Officer at Bunge, a world leader in sourcing, processing, and supplying oilseed and grain products and ingredients. Deborah is a seasoned HR and business executive who has enabled business success through people for over twenty years. Her record of success can be attributed to an unusual breadth of experience having held key leadership roles in both general management and Human Resources for over twenty years in multinational industry leading companies.*

Journal Entry
November 11, 2040

Dear journal,

I've thought about this day for a long time, and it's finally here. I've thought long and hard about how I could create purpose and meaning in retirement. About how I could continue to be mentally and socially engaged when I didn't have a standard workplace consuming sixty-plus hours of my week. About how my professional experiences and best-practices have changed and evolved over the past four-plus decades of my life.

As I got to thinking, I found it rather stunning just how much our definition of work has changed over these years and what it's meant for HR professionals like myself. I had a great chance to reflect on this during my commute into work. Speaking of, the task of getting to work has changed so much. The quiet of the commute coupled with the absence of traffic has meant a far faster trip into my shared work space environment that I call my office, but it's also a more peaceful one. Autonomous transportation has enabled speed and brought a lot more peace to the beginning of one's day.

I remember spending my days as the Chief HR Officer for a number of large multinational companies, where a central theme was to continually reinvent strategies, programs, policies, and practices to ensure my organization would be able to adapt to the ever-changing requirements of work. Changing demographics, societal and technological demands were changing many elements of the workplace, and workplaces themselves were changing.

The prime of my career was a period where we saw a rise in small cap companies. I attribute this in part, at least in the US, to the social uprising around short-term capital deployment and the resurgence of labor unions. Short-term shareholder capital gave rise to activism and pressure on companies to perform better, faster, and more consistently. This period of time saw the spin-off of many smaller companies, fewer conglomerate business models, and more niche, "pure play" entities. The performance pressure that emerged in this period also drove actions within companies from control mechanisms to restructurings that changed cultures and modified the employer-employee relationship over a period of time.

The changing view of long-term security with an employer, and the emerging landscape of new types of companies that were forming were key factors to the rise of the independent worker. Today, compared to twenty years ago, more people have chosen to work for themselves and have multiple employers.

This has been aided, in part, by the changes in social and labor protection that became increasingly important to protect the new class of gig workers. Fluid work schedules and changes in employment constructs required a new legislative framework to slowly emerge over the years. While these types of workers are not the majority today as was once viewed as a sure certainty, they do form a large part of the labor market and it's impressive to see how much has changed in the regulatory space to ensure their rights are protected.

Increased life spans have also clearly created a change in the working population. People are working longer, which means there are more people in the workforce competing for work. The notion of the job for life has very much been replaced by the emergence of short-term contracts. There are far more people today being employed for a specific task or outcome in more specialized, shorter stints of work. In the past, this work was performed more regularly by consulting firms who would augment the permanent workforce and the skills it represented for a specific project, turnaround, or deliverable. Today, the same concept exists, but these people are independent workers who are woven much more into the fabric of the company, with little that distinguishes them from someone on a longer term or undefined tenure employment contract.

In companies, the notion of employment at will expanded with these various changes in society and the workplace. Many employees are making transitions every three to five years to adjacent companies, customers, and competitors, and many of these transitions are being facilitated by their employers. Companies are playing a larger role in providing cross-company opportunity for their employees—with fluid contracts of employment allowing for a value proposition of career growth and maintaining one's interest for a lifelong career. People change jobs more today than they did in the past, but the communities of people in the working world feel smaller, more connected.

These demographic shifts created the need to rethink the definition of success in one's talent base. The availability of talent for roles was becoming restricted when traditional definitions of success criteria were overlayed with prospective talent. Companies like the one I worked for became more focused on the specific skills required in a role that could be earned through life experience and/or various certifications versus being solely focused on a four-year university degree.

Unfortunately, changes in the education sector have been marginal, and the new skill-based currency is still not reflected in four-year university programs. People have adapted by re-skilling themselves thanks in part to programs provided by institutional employers, and in part due to the availability of private institutions offering shorter, targeted curriculum. I smile when I think about the re-emergence and appreciation of skilled trades. The apprentice-based programs we have now have saved skills, like jewelry-making and welding, that were nearing extinction a few years ago.

I remember the rapid digital and technological change that brought in a new level of competition and threatened the very fabric of our business model. I recall the rise of the digital era where everything became suddenly available with one tap on a handheld device, and how 'app' became a standard word in our vocabulary. In what felt like the blink of an eye, we transformed from a world where data points were few and far between and backward-looking to one where information is available and actionable in real-time and can be used to predict future realities.

The rise of automation and artificial intelligence (AI) has morphed the shape of work, but not in the drastic way I once feared. Certainly, some skills have been replaced by automation, digitalization, and machine-learning, but new roles have also emerged in this process. The morphing of work opened space for a more skill-based approach to role and organizational design, breaking down jobs into a series of activities and skills, and reassembling roles with the skills that could not get replaced by technology and automation. The human dimension of work has taken significant prominence, and we have seen the rise of disciplines, such as psychology and neuroscience, as companies, entrepreneurs, and academics have more intently focused on understanding the complex innerworkings of the human mind. There are far more jobs today focused on the human dimension, such as nursing, coaching, and caring. Jobs that, given their very nature, require empathy—an art that we have not yet seen replaced by technology.

As information became ubiquitous, companies of all types became data-centric—with information access, availability, and protection becoming a core premise to business success. This allowed new disciplines to emerge—many focused on swiftly mining data to generate insights. Companies re-focused their training platforms to build analytic skills across companies and focused the employee experience on setting leadership expectations and developing new and innovative communication methods to reach employees where they are—figuratively and literally. The emergence of the agile workforce created a space for professionals like me to bring even more value to our companies—in bringing a whole new level of thinking to workplace layout and culture.

As I looked around during my commute this morning, I was mindful of the various cafes and social gathering spaces that have sprung up in the places that used to be laden with retail stores. The increasing importance of work environment over the years, and the skill shortage many sectors and disciplines have experienced, has led to a decreased prominence on when and where people work. And it shifted the importance we place on being agile around where and how work gets performed. I spent a large portion of my career advocating for and creating flexible work arrangements and office policies that enabled collaboration, sharing of ideas, and freedom for people to create, think, and perform at times that worked best for them.

Today, the sharing economy whether it be housing, transportation, work spaces, clothing, or a multitude of other sectors where access is gained through subscription or a sharing model, is far more prominent than owning outright as it was in my day. Although these trends have had profound impacts on the world of work, I think they have made it all the better. There are fewer traditional jobs the way I remember there to be, but there are many ways of earning a good solid living, and plenty ways of generating purpose in one's life. And I feel that today we are more driven by purpose as a society than I ever recall it being before.

And that brings me to my retirement and what it will look like. The notion of retirement has shifted given so many of the standards around work have shifted. For me, as I head into the next phase of my life, I see a portfolio career of my own emerging. My speaking and consulting will enable me to share my rich and vast leadership experiences over the last forty years in three continents. I'll take advantage of the advent of micro-learning by reproducing some of my content and using my network of seasoned leaders and well-known personalities, to generate bite-size learning content that is accessible to the masses. And more importantly, recognized by companies as valid education for skill building necessary in today's competitive world. I will continue with the investment and advisory work I've been doing in the start-up world, particularly for women-owned start-ups. Supporting women's success will remain a pinnacle of what brings me purpose. And finally, in retirement, I look forward to taking advantage of the sharing economy as my ownership of material things minimizes, freeing me to travel around the world to places that I have imagined visiting for many years.

And most of all, during retirement, I look forward to seeing how work continues to emerge and evolve—and how we as a society adapt to what's ahead. Our future will indeed be bright.

Gene Holtzman *is an innovator of the recruiting and staffing industry. He started Mitchell Martin, a technology staffing firm in 1983 and has grown the business to over $200 million in revenue. Recently, he co-founded Talent Tech Labs, a startup incubator and consulting firm focused on talent acquisition technology.*

Written with: **Josh Holtzman** *is the co-founder of InterviewJet, a digital staffing platform and a co-founder of Talent Tech Labs.*

Career Path Described by Sophia Robles
A Graduate of the Class of 2040

Hello, my name is Sophia Robles, and I have just graduated today, May 30, 2040. I am going to tell you about my career path; how it started and where I think my career will ultimately end up landing.

First, let me start by giving you some context of how I got to where I am today.

My parents came to the US in 2030 when I was only eleven years old. My mother and father were both awarded a merit-based visa sponsored by the company Salesforce. Salesforce paid the US government $20,000 for each of my parents since they had technical skills that there was a shortage of in the United States. This visa program and increased visa quota were made possible by the group behind Ideal Immigration. They ultimately were able to convince politicians to start inviting more talent with certain skills to the United States and have companies pay the government $20,000 per hire, similar to how they paid recruiting fees in the past for hard-to-find talent. Because my parents were part of this new immigration program, my family was able to come to the US.

Growing up, my parents made it clear to me that you are only as good as your last project and that I should always be working on new things to build and sharpen my skill set. I have been working since I was legally able to, at thirteen. My first "job" was a little different from jobs I heard of in the past, like working in a restaurant or lifeguarding for the summer. My first job was working on simple tasks for five cents each that I found on Amazon Mechanical Turk. I went to Amazon's Mechanical Turk homepage, put in my information, and started working on tasks. Finding my first job was as simple as that. That first day, I did over 350 different tasks and made $17.50. All my tasks the first day were centered around data entry. One example was to look up a business's address online and enter the information. Each and every task was different, and the instructions were written clearly in the task description, so the tasks didn't require any pre-training. I inputted data in a designated field to complete the task. As I received great online reviews on my tasks, I "unlocked" new opportunities and started being able to work on more complicated projects. One of these was to review an artificial intelligence bot and the experience it provided. My job was to help train the bot to better service users. I would say or ask the bot certain things and grade how helpful the bot was.

This specific job led me to do private learning on how artificial intelligence worked while I was in in high school. As a result, my grades suffered a bit, but I learned a lot more practical and cutting-edge skills. I watched videos online and took cheap classes on sites like Udemy. I built relationships with the teachers and eventually started competing in data science competitions on Kaggle.com. At the beginning I didn't have much luck winning any of the competitions, but I did start to meet people through the competitions. Over time a group of us started to build synergies working together and won our first competition, which awarded each of us $5000. We helped the NFL solve a data issue with player stats they were having. All of a sudden, we hit a winning streak and started winning many of Kaggle's competitions for supporting various different companies. This got the attention of investors. Instead of investing in our group to build a company, they actually invested in us as individuals. They funded our education and in return earned 5 percent of our salary until the original investment was paid back in full plus a 14 percent return per year. This is called an income share agreement program, which was designed and administered by Vemo Education and sponsored by the investor Softbank. I used this investment toward an education at a one-year data science vocation school and a three-year degree from Carnegie Mellon's Artificial Intelligence School.

One perk of the income share agreement was that after graduation, if I worked at a company that Softbank's Vision Fund invested in, every $1 I earned would actually count as $2 toward paying back my income share.

This would help immensely in lessening the amount of time it took to pay off my obligation and making my money 100 percent free and clear. Obviously, they did this to retain talent in their ecosystem.

In addition to the opportunities through Softbank, Carnegie Mellon has also provided me offers at six different companies, but I doubt I am going to accept any of them.

Carnegie Mellon gets presigned commitments each year from companies to make a certain number of hires from each of their departments. Since post-graduation is now highly rated on the US News College Ranking System, getting students hired is very important to them. Many colleges have even outsourced their career centers to experienced staffing firms to provide better service and increase placement rate.

And now here I am today, a graduate of Carnegie Mellon with a huge portfolio of projects and tasks that I have worked on. I have no student debt, but I do have to pay the 5 percent portion of my salary to Vemo/ Softbank every year.

Now that I have completed my "formal education" it is time look for my first real long-term gig. I am more interested in the type of project than the particular company but know picking the right company could bring on additional projects of interest. Instead of how, in the past, people either decided to be a temporary worker or full-time employee, there is a new category called committed freelancers. I will commit to only one engagement at a time, and I will dedicate approximately forty hours a week to that company. The engagements typically will last six to eight months. Some will renew for more time, and others I will move on from to a new adventure! I have my own LLC, and I am technically responsible for my own healthcare benefits and 401(k) plan, but I use a third party that pools a bunch of freelancers together to get better rates and handles the administration.

I have my own career portal provided by my staffing firm that manages all my work. The portal tracks companies that are interested in hiring me, education and skill verification, my professional work and projects that I have worked on in the past, and the feedback that my superiors have provided about my work. It also includes my availability for projects, my target compensation, and tax tracking.

Today I went to my career portal and moved my status from passive to active. All of a sudden, a lot of opportunities started coming in. Some of these opportunities are coming directly from companies, but many are also coming from my talent agent. My talent agent reviews all inquiries before they are passed on to me. They remove the ones that are not the right fit for me, whether that is because of skill set, compensation, or location. My talent agent also writes special notes that are viewable in my career portal, giving me her thoughts and recommendations as well as a deadline for next steps. Sometimes my talent agent will even do an initial call on my behalf to collect more details about the opportunity. The transcripts of the calls are recorded in my career portal so that I can review the information and how my agent is representing me.

Based on today's options, I am likely to pick a seven-month algorithm redesign project with Automation Anywhere. My logic is that they have one of the largest real-time data sets and since they are part of the Softbank family, every dollar is really $2 toward my income share agreement.

Assuming I accept this opportunity, you may be wondering: What is next for me?

While I am working on this project, my talent agent will be scouting out my next gig so that I will not have any downtime. My agent will also be recommending ongoing training classes and introductions to mentors that will help develop my skills and continue to make me more marketable. Some of the classes are actually paid for by software companies, where they not only teach me new skills, but also show me how to use their tools. These software companies use this as a competitive advantage to sell their software, as the more people who are trained on using it, the more sense it makes for a company to align with that software. I am thrilled to get paid to continue to learn new things! I even get certifications verifying my skills.

I plan to live in over ten different cities through my career. I will switch on and off, working onsite versus working remotely. Sometimes I will take assignments that may pay less but will help me learn more. When I sign on for these projects, I will try to work in tertiary cities like Nashville and Charlotte to lower my living expenses.

I will judge and measure myself on productivity gains from my efforts. In the past, having a number of people reporting to you was a "badge of honor"; today it is all about how much positive change my efforts bring. I don't care if I run a team with two people or fifty, as long as the impact is made. In many of my projects I will actually manage a combination of both people and bots. People are expensive but can understand and navigate change well. Bots are cheap and scalable but don't do so well with change.

Ultimately, I will retire, but I don't think I will ever fully stop "working." To keep busy, I will teach online classes, mentor others and help validate their skills, join the gig economy to do simple tasks, and continue to earn income for my family. Every day is new....

Gene Zaino, *an avid entrepreneur and nationally recognized expert in the next way of working, launched MBO Partners to reinvent the way independent consultants and organizations work together. For more than twenty years, he has helped MBO to lead the charge and keep the independent economy moving forward, building a unique, dual-sided ecosystem comprising many of the world's most prominent companies and in-demand professionals.*

To My Firstborn Granddaughter, Abigail.

2040 seems so far off, yet also just around the bend. Will you have chosen a career? Built your own business? Gone to college or pursued a trade? Found love or traveled the world? Only time will tell what you will do with this great big wonderful life you've been given—but one thing is for sure: the future is uncertain yet an exciting adventure for all of us. The surest path to success is the one we forge ourselves, through hard work, passion, and dedication.

When I was asked to write this chapter, I immediately thought of you. It's hard to believe that in 2040, you'll be twenty-one, fresh with possibilities about what your future might look like.

Independents: Less Jetsons, More Iron Man

When I imagined working in the future as a child, I recall watching *The Jetsons*—a cartoon series set far, far in the future, where people drove flying cars, 3-D printed their food, and talked to anyone anywhere in the world via a smartwatch. (Funny enough, many of these inventions once thought of as "Space Age" are available today.)

But there's one thing *The Jetsons* never predicted—that people wouldn't work for companies like Spacely Sprockets but, rather, for themselves. Over the past twenty years, the rapid rise of the independent workforce has created new opportunities and challenges to our economy and society, and I am certain it will continue to be a major force impacting our lives in the next twenty years as well. By the time you start working, more than half of the workforce will be, or will have been at some point in their career, self-employed.

That's why I like to use another analogy. The future doesn't look like the Jetsons, where people went about their daily lives and jobs using technology simply for convenience. Instead, we will see people creatively combine a treasure trove of technologies, data, and resources to build their own productive version of an *Iron Man* suit, giving them the power of independence to pursue their passion and financial well-being.

In 2040, savvy individuals will use technology to work smarter, to work more productively, and to protect themselves and their careers against obsolescence as they leverage these resources to make themselves—and their work—more valuable. These skills and tools make you powerful, creating an armor, just like an *Iron Man* suit, that will insulate you and let you do things you've never imagined.

Self-employment in 2040 will look very little like it looks today. I'd love to offer you some unfiltered advice and predictions about what the world may look like then and the twists and turns to get there.

The Next Way of Working Is Here—but What Does That Mean?

Today, in 2020, we stand on the precipice of the next way of working. Nearly forty-one million Americans[13] embrace the independent lifestyle either full- or part-time. Satisfaction among independents is the highest it's ever been. In less than five years, more than half of the workforce will experience self-employment at some point in their careers, and many will cycle back and forth between self-employment and traditional employment in years to come. By the time you turn twenty-one, this number will rise to more than 60 percent, if not higher. Traditional retirement won't be the goal either. You'll invest in new endeavors, to keep your skills fresh and your income diversified, as well as to fulfill your passions and find your purpose.

But growth hasn't always been—and won't always be—easy. While this type of work grows rapidly, we increasingly tell the "tale of two independents" as the largest areas of expansion exist at the high and low ends of

---

13 *MBO Partners, State of Independence in America 2019*, https://www.mbopartners. com/state-of-independence.

the income spectrum. On one hand, we see a rapid rise in commodity platforms, where buyers primarily engage independents to perform an undifferentiated service (driving a car, walking a dog) and workers generally receive their assignments from an app-based algorithm to generate extra income, fill a gap between jobs or other gigs, or pursue independent work just as a way to meet new people and socialize. But app-based algorithms of commodity services can soon create a race to the bottom for wages. People who need to rely solely on this type of work will find it hard to make ends meet, and society will need to create a new social safety net for independents to prevent income deterioration, similar to minimum-wages rules in traditional employment.

On the other hand, a strong jobs market and an increasing skills gap have led many highly skilled and creative workers to leap into independence as a way to make more money while enjoying flexibility and lifestyle benefits that can be hard to come by as traditionally employed individuals. It is this portion of the workforce that I believe will be most successful, both in the immediate and long-term future. In contrast to the need for a safety net, policies need to encourage, and enable, people to work independently, giving them the freedom to build their skills, to be happier, and to know that they are a productive contributor to society. It will be important to carefully balance these two conflicting policy vectors. Too much of a protectionist environment will inhibit the use of Independent Workers, taking away the freedom to choose to take on the risks and rewards inherent in independent work.

As skilled independent labor continues to grow, organizations will place a premium not just on the workers themselves, but also on the results and successes driven from the projects independents complete. It is here that the model of working in the future will really begin to change, as we move from a traditional workforce to a fractionalized one where work itself is packaged as a product to be purchased, rather than paid for by the hour. This will be the first step to freeing up time as Independent Workers leverage their *Iron Man* suits to deliver results, rather than merely services. Imagine being a one-person business that can outsource work to others, use robots and artificial intelligence to make new creations, and collaborate with multiple buyers of what you produce. Maybe you can place much of this on autopilot, giving you more time to live life.

Skilled and creative independent professionals will fill needs for both in-demand skills not currently present in a company's full-time employee (FTE) population, as well as to help complete projects—both strategic and tactical—that need additional people to meet aggressive timelines to keep up with a fast-paced, changing environment. Attracting and building relationships with independent talent has become a strategic and important aspect of a company's workforce. I predict this trend will continue, with companies articulating a specific value statement for independents within their greater talent strategy similar to, or even more enhanced than, their fulltime recruiting strategy.

By 2040, organizations will assemble their workforces with both independents and FTEs, with equal weight and value placed on both parts of the workforce mix. The companies that do this best will have a leg up on their competition.

It's Going to Get Hard (Before It Gets Better)

It's easy to think that the next generation reaps the benefits of generations before. While that's true to a point, and while I hope that your road to success is easy, the path will have its twists and not-so-welcome turns.

In the coming years, for the first time ever, we'll see four generations actively engaged in the same workforce, from the new Gen Z workers to millennials to Gen Xers and boomers. Much has been written about what this melding will cause...and it won't be easy.

Many boomers are unprepared for retirement and will draw on resources like Social Security and Medicare with a heavy hand, putting enormous stress on our economy.

We're heading toward a tipping point, one where our present burdens will cause a fundamental shift not just in how we work but also in how we think of social responsibility.

Today's employment system is broken, and it has been for some time. Workers no longer leave a company after fifty years with a pension and a gold watch. They no longer build careers at one or two companies. Whether traditionally employed or working as an independent, people no longer can rely on their employers to deliver them core benefits like health insurance, retirement savings programs, career development, and more. Today, however, our policies, systems, and behaviors rely on employment to deliver these core social safety nets. This must and will change, but it will be challenging along the way.

Employers need to think in the same manner. They position their most valuable asset as their "people," treating their full-time workforce to benefits like health care and paid leave, offering training opportunities and valuable development benefits. But they often sideline their most strategic assets—their contract workforce population—by treating them like second-class citizens.

The media and government cry foul, bemoaning a race to the bottom, when in fact, satisfaction and choice among independents have never been higher.

The tipping point won't be pretty. I believe before we can move toward a world where independents are seen as a valued economic and entrepreneurial asset, we'll swing the other way in an attempt to protect a broken world of work.

Then, to add to this, there are the economic cycles. Based on population demographics, the debt balance of our economy, and others around the world, we will see a nasty recession in the early 2030s. This will be a rough economic period for a few years, where companies will make major workforce reductions, reducing traditional employment by the millions… but then this will be the genesis to a new and exciting way to work.

Here, the millennial generation rises to the top of the workforce food chain, initiating a new culture of work: where independence is favored. This is what I call the rise of the Maker Force, and the decline of the labor-based workforce.

The Rise of the Maker Force

The rise of this Maker Force will be a way for people to take advantage of great tools, fulfill passions, and make money not just based on time, but on leveraging skills and assets, be they data, software tools, or physical goods. Creativity will reign, and consumers will benefit from a thriving global economy.

What's a maker, you ask? Makers are those who leverage more than just labor, time, and materials for their jobs. Makers take their knowledge and produce an asset that can derive value, and with that value, income, both now and in the future. Examples of this include writing a book, selling a song, creating a new service, or investing in productive assets like real estate or software, as well as traditional methods of making a product for sale (perhaps on Etsy or some new marketplace).

You'll earn your living based not just on a flat, transactional skill set, but based on your intellectual property and your personal brand, a concept previously reserved only for companies, and your income-generating potential and value to the market will grow accordingly.

Today, savvy companies are investing in this type of talent. Grow with Google[14] is helping train for jobs with skills-based learning programs and tools; the program has helped more than ten million people to date. That's a quarter of the total independent workforce in 2019!

Amazon, the business behemoth that started as little more than an online bookstore, is now giving people $10,000 to start their own delivery-based business.[15]

These companies know that incentivizing and championing entrepreneurial makers is the key to success, but they still have a long way to go.

In the coming years, the tools we have to perform, optimize, and complete work will grow faster than we've ever imagined. This technology will be the rocket fuel we need to help today's consultants become the Maker Force of tomorrow.

Savvy independents will team up with each other to leverage relationships, to capitalize on shared intellectual property, and to fractionalize work, so that income will be a separate concept from "hours worked."

We all have twenty-four hours in a day. To live your best life, you can't work all the time. The way to do that is to create something—or many

14 Grow with Google website, https://grow.google/about/.

15 Louise Matsakis, "Why Amazon Is Giving Employees $10,000 to Quit," *Wired*, May 14, 2019, https://www.wired.com/story/amazon-delivery-paying-employees-to-quit/.

things—that generate income, knit them together, and create a consumable product or service.

In order to achieve this state, you must have other things producing income for you. Figure out how to knit it together and create something that is consumable, just as many of the world's most successful businesses do today. Thanks to AI, technology, and shifting workforce demographics, you'll be able to leverage a unique opportunity: to become a maker in the micro business economy—the independent workforce of the future—taking your ideas, passion, and talents and selling them back to the workforce not just as a worker bee in someone else's hive, but as a thriving business of one.

The Skills You Need to Succeed

Success tomorrow isn't about the one thing you can do today, but about the little things you can do every day to prepare you every day. The biggest tool you can bring to the workforce of tomorrow is a creative and open mind. Learn what your God-given talent is. Find out what you can develop and do better than anyone else. Find your purpose and live it.

There are so many possibilities—the hard part will be narrowing down what drives you.

Here, your entrepreneurial skills will matter. You'll need to be alert to what's going on around you and also have the creativity and confidence to do something that's not been done before or the vision to do it in a better way.

Building your own business isn't always comfortable, nor does it come with a rulebook. You'll need to trust your gut, as well as be a bit of an anthropologist. Study others. Understand what has worked. See where needs arise. You'll need to understand how your unique skills fit in, and where you can bring new, fresh perspectives to the world and leave it a better place than you found it. And if you're savvy, you'll find a way to deliver value to yourself along the way as well.

When I started MBO Partners, I had a vision of making a better world for Independent Workers, of making it easier, more productive, and more lucrative for them to work the way they wanted. In the more than two decades since, I've stayed true to that North Star, that mission.

But I wouldn't have been able to be successful without decisive action. With so many tools and choices at your fingertips, the ability to act on opportunities, to pivot and to respond to change, will become more important than ever.

You need to know how to leverage resources, how to make the most of data available to you, of partnerships, and of what you've learned. How you take those individual points and make something out of them that's valuable not just to yourself, but to others, and improve your life and the lives of others as well. *That's* the dream.

You won't be able to do all this alone. A key failing of technology is that it can make us feel invincible. After all, we can meet, talk, and connect virtually with anyone in the world with the push of a button. But technology is worthless without real, meaningful communication.

At every moment, use the resources around you to help you form deep, meaningful relationships. Talk face-to-face where possible. Listen, really listen, to what others have to say. Communication is one of the most important skills you can learn—among family, friends, and colleagues. Those skills will serve you well in all aspects of business, whether you are bouncing a new idea off a friend, pitching a potential investor, or selling your products or services for the first or fiftieth time.

Those skills can also help you feel less alone when you fail. Communication breeds community, and that community of family, friends, and colleagues will become your safety net when you fail. Note that I say when—not if.

Failure isn't rock bottom, Abigail. It's part of the journey. But as long as you learn from each mistake, each misstep, and each trial, and emerge stronger, more resilient, and more motivated, even if there are tears and skinned knees and struggles along the way, that will be the real success.

And I hope that when you look back twenty or forty or sixty years from now, you find success—coupled with lessons learned along the way—and you can share your own story with the next generation.

2040 seems so far away, but it isn't so very far off after all. I can't wait to see all the places you'll go, and how you'll forge your very own—and very independent—path.

With Love,
Pop G

Holly Paul *is the Chief Human Resources Officer at FTI Consult-*
ing, a global business advisory firm headquartered in Washington,
DC. Ms. Paul leads the efforts to attract, engage, hire, develop, and
retain FTI Consulting's leading professionals. In her role, Ms. Paul
is responsible for overseeing all areas of human capital, including
talent acquisition, talent management, learning and development,
workforce planning, compensation and benefits.

Reflections of a 2040 College Graduate

Graduation was fast approaching. Soon I would don a cap and gown, walk across the stage with the rest of the class of 2040, and exit through the door into the real world that was waiting on the other side.

In the lead-up to this moment, my parents reflected on their grad-uations and subsequent job searches, which typically involved typing up a résumé, emailing it to a company, and then traveling to an office for interviews.

That is so…old-fashioned.

Let me tell you how the job search plays out now. Times have changed so much that I never stepped foot in an office for an interview, let alone typed up a résumé or sent an email. There was no career fair on campus. My job search included video résumés, AI, avatars and chatbots, and a virtual tour of an "office" that was done from my tablet computer at home. My résumé was a thirty-second video clip explaining why I was the right person for the job.

How can thirty seconds on video land you a job, you might ask? Look at it this way. I was on my college debate team. I was applying for jobs in management consulting. The ability to see both sides of an issue and pres-ent my positions with coherent, convincing arguments was a significant plus. My video résumé let me tell the story of how I managed travel for debate team meets with my coursework, while still maintaining time for volunteering at the local food bank and playing for a club soccer team. I could write about my experience, but showing it let me tell a better story about how I could take my skills and apply them to the job at hand.

Tailoring my skills to the particular job I applied for made all the difference. Companies are using AI to help them vet applicants. AI scans all applications and résumés and identifies the ones that most closely match the job requirements, performing a task that took recruiters weeks in mere minutes. It uses algorithms to determine if a candidate is telling the truth, examining vocal inflection and body language. If I couldn't explain how I could help the company and succeed in the position—and convince the AI tool that I was being honest—my video résumé would go in the virtual dustbin.

This new era spawned a new way to prepare for interviews, done right from an app on my phone. I sat down in front of my smartphone or tablet, opened up an app, and started filming my résumé. The same AI tools a company used to evaluate my résumé and application offered me feedback and a likely score of how my application would compare to other candidates, right there on the spot. I used that feedback to craft the perfect messages for my résumé.

After I submitted my résumé to the company, I received an email with a link to join an interview. This was an encouraging first step. In my parents' day, a recruiter would have conducted this interview by phone. But when I clicked the link, I was staring face to face with…an avatar. This bot did the initial screening using AI to evaluate my responses to questions and compare them to the job requirements for the position. Even though there was not a person on the other end, I still found it to be stressful. I needed to make sure I was properly enunciating and repeating my key messages about why I was the right fit for the job. This would help the AI tool recognize my qualifications and hopefully put me in the mix for the role.

Much to my relief, I moved on to the next stage of interviews. This required me to meet with team members and managers in London, Hong Kong, New York, and San Francisco. Yet, there was one problem, I thought—I live in Chicago. Just out of college. With no money. How would I afford to travel to these locations? I briefly pondered declining the opportunity before I was told that these interviews would be done from my computer as well, via video. However, instead of meeting with an avatar again, I would speak live with actual people. In fact, most of these people worked remotely and had not seen the inside of an office in quite some time. Work and life appeared to be much more intertwined. One of the people interviewing me worked from home so he could take his kids to dance class after school. Another interviewed me from her local coffee shop after teaching a morning yoga class. While videoconferences still lack the personal touch of an in-person meeting, it was nice to interact with human beings after dealing with apps, avatars, and bots at the beginning of the process.

These interviews also offered the opportunity to ask the more prob-ing questions about how these employees viewed their work, what they thought of the company and its culture, and how they could see me fitting in. With all the technology in the interview process, asking those questions became even more imperative. For me and many of my peers, a company's values were a main selling point. We wanted to see those values infused in everything a company does. Understanding how a company's values match my own helped me determine whether I could see myself working there.

After several days of waiting, I received a phone call. I got the job! And the best part, I didn't have to move anywhere. I could do it right from my apartment in Chicago. My employer mailed me a computer and video camera. I set up my home office, a spartan space with a few family photos on the bookcase behind me. I wanted to make sure it at least looked like a legitimate office to my new coworkers. I also needed professional attire on hand. Even though I would be working remotely, I would have to look presentable on camera or if I did have to travel.

My first day started like many others would. I woke up, went to the gym, put on a new suit, and flipped open my brand-new laptop. Next on the agenda was a tour of my new company's office. But everyone works remotely, so how can there be an office, you ask? It's simple. Each employee chooses an avatar—it can resemble their likeness or something completely different. Then we log in to a virtual reality program that places us in an "office." We gather around a conference table, and I introduce myself through a combination of audio dialogue and text chat. A video function is also available to see colleagues face-to-face. There even was a welcome party by a virtual "ping pong table." I still haven't figured out how to get my avatar to play ping pong, however.

The interview process certainly was convenient, doing it from the comfort of my home, but it was no less stressful. I needed to make sure my responses would satisfy the AI algorithms. I had to conduct my due diligence on the company, its culture and growth opportunities. I still needed to impress the hiring managers.

And yet I can only imagine that someday, hearing this story about my first job interview, my children will tell me how old-fashioned I sound.

The views expressed herein are those of the author(s) and not necessarily the views of FTI Consulting, Inc., its management, its subsidiaries, its affiliates, or its other professionals.

Ian Ziskin *is president of EXec EXcel Group, LLC, where he serves as a board advisor, coach, consultant, entrepreneur, teacher, speaker, and author. He is also co-founder and partner of Business inSITE Group (BiG), a strategic partnership focused on coaching, leadership development, and HR transformation. Ian's global business experience includes Chief Human Resources Officer and other senior leadership roles with three Fortune 100 corporations—Northrop Grumman, Qwest Communications, and TRW.*

The Future of Work and Leadership
10 Predictions, 3 Trends, and 5 Capabilities

It is virtually impossible to predict the future of anything. Yet, that does not stop many of us from being intoxicated by "what *it* will be like *when*...." I have spent my entire career thinking about the "it" and "when" associated with key changes and challenges in work, the workforce, and the workplace. The past, present, and future of work have profound implications, not only for the people who *do* the work, but also for the people who *lead* those who do the work.

This essay suggests ten specific predictions, highlights three emerging trends, and recommends five new capabilities that leaders must master to successfully address these predictions and trends over the next twenty years—by the year 2040. The most intriguing question is not "will *all* these things happen?" The real question is "when *any* of these things happen, will leaders be ready and relevant to address them?"

10 Predictions

By the year 2040, the world of work in the United States will be characterized by the following realities:

1) 50 percent of the workforce will be in freelance, gig, or other agile and nontraditional roles, not in specific jobs working for specific organizations...and they will deliver their work through a combination of

virtual and/or flexible work arrangements that include locations and schedules of their choice.

2) 50 percent of board of directors' seats will be held by women and people of color.

3) 33 percent of company CEOs will be women or people of color.

4) 100 percent of the workforce will be covered by health care and retirement plans that are completely portable, thereby allowing talent to move freely and seamlessly among and across organizations and work assignments.

5) Mandatory retirement will be completely abolished for all but the most safety-critical jobs.

6) The fastest-growing jobs and gigs in the manufacturing and technology sectors will be associated with artificial intelligence, climate change, data sciences, health care, high-speed transport, machine learning, and robotics.

7) 25 percent of high school graduates will opt to move on to technical apprenticeship programs, rather than to college or directly to work.

8) More people will complete formal credentialing programs in leadership each year than will receive MBA degrees.

9) Leadership Effectiveness Scores for individual leaders and leadership teams will be as commonplace and transparent as Yelp ratings.

10) At least 50 percent of the next six US presidents will be African American, Asian, Latinx, LGBTQ, Jewish, Muslim, and/or women.

3 Trends

Even if only half of the above predictions come to pass, there are clear implications for a host of underlying trends that are emerging around the future of work. Here are the three that will matter most:

▶ **Agile On-Demand Talent**—more agile talent and more flexible organization models are inevitable. There will be more gigs and fewer traditional jobs as defined by current employment models. Increased flexible and virtual work arrangements will be the norm, including many situations where leaders and the people they lead never meet in person. Workers will work on what they want, when they want, where they want, and with whom they want. Increasingly, this trend will be driven by workforce demands and expectations, irrespective of whether company strategies prefer to embrace more traditional definitions of work or organizational operating models. The people strategy will be defined first and foremost by the people, not by the organization.

▶ **Technology-Enabled Work and Workforce**—expertise in and comfort with algorithms, artificial intelligence, and automation as well as human-machine collaboration will permeate nearly every industry, skill set, and functional discipline. Humans will be replaced by computers, machines, and robots in many jobs and industries. Likewise, entire new industries and skill demands will create unprecedented new opportunities for millions of people. But the skills available in the workforce will not align with the new technologies and capabilities required—at least not easily or right away. Big disruption is ahead, including unemployment, job dislocation, and skills shortages. Big opportunity is also ahead, including new industries, new industrial policy, and new large-scale learning and skill-development programs.

▶ **Economic and Social Polarization**—climate, crime, demographics, diversity, drugs, education, food, health, inequality, politics, population, race, religion, unemployment, urbanization, and war are just a handful of global issues confronting organizations and societies. Big-picture problems like these and others require big-picture solutions, which in turn require big-picture leaders. While the issues themselves are hugely complex, they are not the most difficult thing to fix. The toughest challenge to address is polarization, and solutions demand sophistication, nuance, and resilience—to get past differences and focus on collaboration and common ground. Those who can articulate problems are in plentiful supply. However, people and organizations that can effectively resolve problems are in pitifully short supply and will be in unprecedented demand over the next twenty years and beyond.

5 Capabilities

The above predictions and trends suggest some fascinating questions about the role, relevance, and readiness of leaders in 2040. What will leaders need to know and do as the future of work emerges? Will leadership be a necessary evil or a strategic differentiator? Will leaders lead people, or robots, and/or work for people, or robots? Will leaders even exist?

For purposes of this essay, I would like to focus on five of my favorite leadership capabilities that will be essential over the next twenty years:

1) **External, *Not* Internal**—in 2040, leaders will distinguish themselves more through their savvy about external trends and dynamics (competitive landscape, economic and social challenges, and other forces of change) than through their deep knowledge of their organization's internal environment (strategy, operations, products, services, and culture). Of course, internal knowledge and experience will always matter. But the ability to master the meaning of external forces will matter more. In the past, most leaders became leaders primarily because of their internal expertise. In the future, external savvy will be a more powerful and meaningful capability.

2) **Networks, *Not* Organizations**—in 2040, organizations as we traditionally define them will have largely been replaced by networks as the foundational operating model for how and through whom work will get done. Who you know will still matter. Who you do not know, but need to know and collaborate with, will matter even more. The ability to find these people, build relationships with them, and get them to work on your priorities and projects without bossing or controlling them will be paramount. Organizational walls, boundaries, boxes, ceilings, silos, and the organization charts used to depict them will still exist. But that will not be the way work actually gets

accomplished. Networks and collaborative relationships will drive how work is done. Leaders will need to deliver results through people they do not own, control, manage, or, in some cases, even know.

3) **Segmentation, *Not* Sameness**—in 2040, the workforce and customer base will be significantly more diverse than they are today. Demographics are destiny. Leaders will therefore need to become comfortable with differentiating how they treat people—communication, development, engagement, feedback, rewards, and work assignments will be increasingly customized and personalized to meet the expectations and needs of different workforce segments and pivotal talent. Treating everyone the same will no longer be the definition of fairness. Fairness will instead be defined by treating people as they need and prefer to be treated—differentiated by workforce segment, contribution, performance, and personal value proposition. This leadership capability implies the application of marketing-related principles to solve people-related problems. Mass customization, differentiation, personalization, and segmentation will be in vogue. Treating everyone the same in the name of fairness will increasingly be a cop-out. And ineffective.

4) **Orchestration, *Not* Expertise**—in 2040, most leaders will become leaders because they are great at orchestrating cross-functional, multidisciplinary solutions to big complex problems. The best leaders will no longer be the biggest experts in their field or organization. Technical expertise will be table stakes, not differentiating. Leadership will be more about finding the very best talent and figuring out whether they need to be employees or freelancers, full-timers or part-timers, onsite or halfway around the world, and bringing out the best in them as individual contributors and as team members. The leader will not be "most expert." The leader will be the one who finds and curates the experts needed, from multiple disciplines, to solve multidimensional problems. Leaders will therefore need to become the most collaborative and humble listeners that organizations have ever seen.

5) **Ready Able,** *Not* **Ready Now**—in 2040, talent strategies and succession planning will no longer be aimed at identifying and developing leaders who are "ready now" to move into their next roles. Instead, the leadership succession pipeline will primarily be filled with leaders who demonstrate readiness for the ever-changing world of work. Successful leaders will possess capabilities including being agile and flexible, seeing around corners, connecting the dots between seemingly unconnected things, and moving quickly to where the workforce and workplace are headed instead of holding on to where they have been. "Ready now" implies we already know what is needed for leaders to excel and suggests that future leadership success will be based on what has worked in the past. What happens if the future looks nothing like the past? "Ready able" implies that we are unsure about what will be needed for leaders to succeed and assumes that the best leaders will be those who are able to flex and morph quickly to new and unanticipated future demands.

Jane Oates *is a thought leader in education and workforce issues. Currently the President of WorkingNation, a nonprofit media entity dedicated to telling the stories of solutions for workers, she has previously held senior positions in the legislative and executive branches of government at the state and federal level, including serving as the Assistant Secretary for Employment and Training at the US Department of Labor.*

As we begin the fourth decade of the twenty-first century, it is important to reflect on how the world of getting a job and keeping a job has changed. Universal income and three-day work weeks have not happened, but major changes have occurred within our long-standing systems.

Corporations have continued their engagement across all levels of education. The skills gaps of the twentieth century persist, and business leaders understand that they need to be fully engaged in order to have the talent they need to increase productivity and expand their markets. Jobs are now listed by skill sets, not title, and while titles still exist internally, they play almost no role in hiring. Sectoral alliances exist in almost every region to promote the skills required for in-demand regional jobs.

Secondary and post-secondary education has evolved to better understand the integration of work and learning. High schools around the country routinely offer dual enrollment opportunities, and nearly half of the students enrolled in high school across all socioeconomic levels have earned college credit. Nearly half of high school students have also had an opportunity to work while attending school, participate in a business-led competition, or become employed as an apprentice.

While the number of colleges closing and merging has continued to climb over the last twenty years, it awakened an innovative spirt across higher education. The burden of cost has been reduced as colleges now offer fluid on- and off-ramps enabling learners to stack credentials to acquire knowledge and skills in real-time relative to their work and to pay as they learn. Pioneered in 2018, Income Share Agreements (ISAs) are now an option on every campus. Innovative partnerships with employers, like Education at Work, employ students at campus-based contact centers, and those student workers graduate without debt and often with jobs.

The definition of a job has also changed. Full-time jobs with one employer now represent only 30 percent of the workforce, heavily skewed to the public sector, and the idea of a nine-to-five workday is almost completely a relic of the past. Flexible schedules, remote offices, and short-term, multiuse spaces are the norm. Gig work, once relegated to the creative world and transportation, now is the reality across sectors. Insurance companies have seen the popularity of their suite of products targeting gig workers become the most successful products in their portfolios.

Advanced screening software and the mechanization of job applications have fostered the growth of creative intermediary programs. Talent Path, created in 2018, now provides ten thousand opportunities for job auditions through their staffing model. Talented people of all ages work as consultants until they are offered full-time positions. Other intermediaries facilitate short-term "tryouts" for jobs, weeklong sessions to solve short-term business problems and give employers and potential workers that chance to see companies from the inside.

While recruitment and onboarding got the attention in the twentieth century, now companies are focused on offboarding. As talent decides to retire, businesses large and small are systemically defining mechanisms to take advantage of the expertise of a retiring workforce to continue in part-time advisory or mentoring roles. Research on the productivity of a multigenerational workforce has renewed interest in how the way that things were can really inform the way that things should be in the future.

Probably the most surprising turn of event is the rebirth of unions. Historically known for blue-collar organization, unions now represent most healthcare workers, including long-term care, and have organized workers across the IT, financial services, and engineering spaces. When asked to explain the renewed interest in unions, there was one answer: workers wanted a voice in the future of the sectors they work in. They wanted a stronger role in their own continued education and a seat at the table when discussions were held on further automation, integrating AI into their workplace, and benefit packages. Unions have made sure that their members and machines work well together. While many jobs have been lost to automation, the labor-management teams have embedded a system of continuous learning that allows the human workforce to continuously reskill to qualify for the new jobs created by the improved technological innovations.

Maybe Buckminster Fuller was right. "We are called to be architects of our future, not its victims."

Johnny C. Taylor, Jr., *SHRM-SCP is President and Chief Executive Officer of the Society for Human Resource Management (SHRM), the world's largest HR professional society. He previously served a two-year term as Chair of the SHRM Board of Directors in 2005 and 2006. Mr. Taylor is the immediate past President and Chief Executive Officer of the Thurgood Marshall College Fund, which represents nearly 300,000 students attending public Historically Black Colleges and Universities.*

See next pages.

THE BEST WAY TO PREDICT THE FUTURE WORKPLACE IS TO CREATE IT

7 THINGS LEADERS MUST GET RIGHT TO THRIVE IN THE 2040 WORKPLACE

JOHNNY C. TAYLOR, JR., PRESIDENT & CEO
SOCIETY FOR HUMAN RESOURCE MANAGEMENT

GAINING ACCESS TO NEW TALENT POOLS, KNOWING HOW TO PIVOT, SOURCE, AND RETRAIN WORKERS, AND RECOGNIZING WHEN AND HOW TO RESTRUCTURE YOUR ORGANIZATION SO PEOPLE CAN SUCCEED WITH PURPOSE WILL BE THE INDISPENSABLE SKILLS SUCCESSFUL LEADERS MUST MASTER TO THRIVE IN THE 2040 WORKPLACE.

IN 2040, THE EXPERIENCE ECONOMY AND SOCIAL ECONOMY ARE LONG GONE. YOUR POWER AS A LEADER FLOWS FROM DEEPER RELATIONSHIPS ON YOUR NETWORK, BUT GLOBAL WORKERS WILL BE **DRIVEN BY PURPOSE AND FREEDOM.**

YOUR BIGGEST CHALLENGE ISN'T TECHNOLOGY, INNOVATION, OR EVEN LEADERSHIP: IT WILL BE FINDING, HIRING, AND ENGAGING THE RIGHT TALENT FOR THE RIGHT JOB RIGHT NOW.

IN A BOUNDARYLESS WORLD THERE IS ONLY ONE WORK STATUS— ON THE PROJECT OR NOT. NEW SKILLS AND EXPERIENCES ARE DEVELOPED WITHIN MINUTES OR HOURS. **EVERYONE IS CONNECTED,** AND EVERYONE EVALUATES **LEADERS & EMPLOYERS**

THE DEFINITION OF AN "EXPERT" IS SEEING A PROBLEM, CREATING SOLUTIONS, GETTING PAID FOR IT, AND DOING IT CONSISTENTLY. THIS ENGENDERS AN INSTANT AND ENTREPRENEURIAL TALENT POOL.

EMPLOYERS WILL OPEN THEIR TRAINING TO THE PUBLIC THEN HIRE THOSE WHO PERFORM WELL.

THERE WILL BE DISRUPTION, AS ALWAYS, BUT **LEADERS WITH THE RIGHT TOOLS, TALENT, AND TRAITS WILL BE ABLE TO LEARN AND PIVOT FLUIDLY.**

LEADERS WHO OFFER ON-THE-JOB DEVELOPMENT, BUILD RELATIONSHIPS, AND KEEP PEOPLE ENGAGED AT DEEPER LEVELS WILL ULTIMATELY WIN THE FUTURE OF TALENT.

Kim Seymour *currently serves as the Chief People Officer at WW (formerly Weight Watchers). A demonstrated ability to architect transformation, forge connections, deliver insights, and link talent to strategy have been the hallmarks of Kim's twenty-plus-year HR career. Previously, Kim focused on the development and delivery of impactful human capital strategies in support of ambitious business goals in progressive roles at American Express, Home Depot, and General Electric.*

There's a school in my neighborhood. An elementary school. So most mornings, hundreds of tiny humans walk past my door. They are the literal "Future of Work." I often wonder, what are they being taught in there? What do they think they want to be when they grow up? What will "work" mean to them?

I'm betting that whatever those children's answers are, there has been (or will be) a technological component or enhancement that has redefined that job from what it looks like today. Something that you nor I could likely imagine today, but more likely something that one of them will invent before they even graduate high school.

Any discussion on "The Future of Work" has technology as the catalyst...and quickly wanders into the fear realm. Fear that humans are being replaced. That humans are becoming obsolete. That humans are being disintermediated. But since the technological revolution will march on—much like the industrial one did eons ago—rather than focus on job construct, the more productive focus may be on what else needs to change, how, and when.

Touching lightly on what work will be, on the continuum of the manual to the creative and insightful, the common belief has been that humans who concentrate higher up that chain are less likely to be made redundant by technological solutions. People readily believe that robotics can perform the functions of a line worker, but work requiring judgment or creativity may be the safe space. Well, AI and machine learning have disproven that time and again already and will only get "smarter."

So where do people fit in? The obvious answer may be that someone has to conceive the technology. Someone has to identify the problem to be solved, someone has to write the code or algorithm, someone has to inter-pret the data, someone has to use the data to make decisions.

There is this phenomenon now where every company is defining itself (or redefining itself) as a tech company. Lofty though they may be, those state-ments are not entirely incorrect. In order to meet customers where they are and provide the experiences that they now expect, the maker of even the most homespun product must figure out how to connect with them. The resulting hiring trajectory across the board is more coders, more specialized program-ming languages, more cloud computing, more e-commerce, more gamifica-tion, more data scientists, and more designers, and this hiring trajectory has outpaced the available talent. So, companies are not hiring less, they are hiring differently. If companies are investing in human resources, it is definitely in these areas. Not doing so means imminent irrelevance.

I would tell those kids that it certainly wouldn't be a bad idea to be technologically proficient. At something. At anything.

For those of us already in the existing workforce, technology should be a galvanizing force. We can embrace how new functionalities can free us from the more mundane and tactical and allow us to focus on creating unique solutions and insights. Becoming the "translator" of enabling tech-nology will be an important role of the future.

All this being said, I think less about what jobs will look like. I think much more about the ancillary items. As "work" changes—how it morphs, what it entails—important adjacent items must also change.

Health care, life insurance, retirement savings, long-term career, dis-ability—societal benefits in some countries—in the US are still tightly linked to an employer and not necessarily (or easily, cheaply, portably) to the employee. Even if the entire workforce doesn't ever fully tilt toward a TaskRabbit-like, gig-focused existence, at the very least average tenure at any one company is likely to continue to decrease. Healthcare benefits are routinely interrupted, reset, or changed by company moves. Econo-mies of scale usually are not available without the negotiating power of a collective. Reliance on company-provided life insurance can risk financial exposure for families in the wake of a death. Some retirement savings plans are not easily transferred and tracked. In short, service providers are pro-viding products for the corporate lifers of the past and have not yet crafted affordable solutions for a very mobile workforce that may have more in common with entrepreneurs. Not figuring this out in an accessible way could have very real health and economic consequences. Those kids passing my house every morning are a long way from having to think about this.

Another ancillary aspect to be concerned about is bias. Many people actually think that bias and discrimination become less of a concern with technological encroachment. Fallacy, according to some. Technology—how it is conceived, programmed, and coded—is still influenced by human beings. Inherent bias in modalities like facial recognition and search results will be perpetuated as long as diversity is lacking in those who create these solutions. Fairness and inclusion are at stake as much as it ever was.

The potential widening of the socioeconomic gap also requires proactive attention, if not intervention. Facility with and accessibility to that "language" is a must. Will schools in disadvantaged areas have the crucial access to computers and instruction that more prosperous neighborhoods have? If not, there is little chance of economic mobility...or even survival. And the spread between the *haves* and the *have-nots* will just get wider.

Another way to approach the question of the future of work is to promote what a *New York Times* article called "a saner way to work." The generational imperative to make careers fit in with your life and not the other way around demands that human resources functions promote greater flexibility to accommodate. Remote work, job shares, more expansive parental leave, fertility coverage, sabbaticals, and more are becoming table stakes. Work is now firmly a life enabler, not a life aspiration. A sense of purpose, interesting work, and flexibility are supplanting the almighty dollar as motivators.

These are not the things that those children walking past my home every day are thinking about right now. But it is coming. It must. "Work" has already evolved since each of us entered the workforce (insert your own decade here). Being a constant learner and adapter is now a necessary skill set. What we know is that the future workplace requires us to understand technology, talk the language of technology, and transform and innovate at an ever-increasing pace.

We can fear this changing landscape, or we can adapt. Technology needs humans. At least right now.

Marcus Sawyerr *is the Founder and CEO of Yoss, a cloud-based talent platform connecting high-demand skills with flexible global opportunities. Marcus has spent time founding (from ideation to revenue at YOSS), investing in (as President of the Adecco Group's Innovation unit, AGX), and advising (in several Board of Director seats and as an active Microsoft Services Executive Board Member) businesses to drive digital transformation and shape the future of work.*

2040 Predictions

As humans, we have a skill to interpret information based on context, experience, and intuition. If we all spend one minute predicting the future, there is a good chance that our predictions will be inaccurate. If we all spend one hour predicting the future, we have a better chance of at least 60 percent accuracy. How long have you spent seriously and intellectually thinking about the future versus listening to the predictions of those who may have spent one minute on the topic? I ask you to spend time thinking about the future not only for yourself and your generation, but also to see if you can connect with your own creative force to shape that future as you would like it to play out.

Now, in order to understand the future, we need to understand how to predict. Predictions are based on accuracy at specific times, and actual experience as well as situational context. Therefore, if we leverage the domain expertise of those who deeply understand statistical analysis, in 2040 we will create more opportunities for all. However, those opportunities may still be divided unequally. To change this narrative, we need to ensure that power becomes more decentralized—and is put in the hands of the people—and that education becomes a utility.

Most people predict that technology will be a major force for innovation and development in the future, and of course they're right. Yet despite the potential impact of technology, our greatest resource is actually our own human skills. Empathy, critical thinking, creativity—that's what make us human, and it will take a very long time for technology to be able to replicate that. If we harness these resources for a purposeful future, things will turn out positively. But if we don't figure out how to use our resources wisely, we might be our own enemies. We, as humans, are more powerful than any AI or disruptive technology today or tomorrow. To help you understand this, I've written something that AI may find challenging to create—and even to read and interpret—twenty years from now:

> The Currency of Purpose. Purpose = society.
>
> Purpose to flourish = purpose to nourish; nourish and nurture = purpose + courage
>
> Division = non-disclosed agenda in conflict, one must surrender
>
> Therefore, no capital gains = societal pains, intellectual wealth uncommonly contained
>
> Multiply abstract green, lush fields scarcely seen, instead organic automation
>
> Whole Foods divided unequally, A-rainforest reigns spectacularly, on-demand
>
> Remote beings, on-demand skills for hire in-demand
>
> Purpose centric decentralized dwellings remain in-demand
>
> Deleting polarization in-demand
>
> Mindful practice on-demand
>
> Outcomes and service on-demand
>
> Ethical roadmaps in-demand
>
> In the end, the people will demand.
>
> -THE END-

What does this all mean!? Let's have a closer look.

At the individual level, if you want to grow, you need to be nourished. But if you want to not just grow but flourish, you need to have courage. And if you want to find purpose in what you do, you need the courage to nourish what you already have. So, if you step back and spend time finding purpose for yourself, that will take courage, but it will also allow you to flourish. Purpose is a core driver of prosperity.

At the political level, what we see at the moment is that we have divided parties and nationalistic systems. Behind these systems lies a hidden modis operandi, and eventually there will be a loser—either humankind or the country. Who's going to be the beneficiary? That nationalist country or the citizen?

Now let's look at the world of business. Businesses are trying to create wealth and achieve capital gains, but if everyone is divided then their plan won't work. If there are no capital gains, it will be society who feels the impact and takes the hit of a boom and bust model. This situation gets worse when the knowledge about how to create wealth *and* support a healthy society is constrained to an elite few. That's where education comes in. We need the crowd to be educated to take things forward in a positive and sustainable way so that profits can be used for a collective good.

What impact will this have on the environment? If we're only focused on making money (multiplying green), and we start automating too many things, we'll lose the foundation of the earth we live on. We need to figure out how to cultivate *real* green fields organically and take care of our earth rather than rampage it.

We live in a world where giants keep getting bigger. Companies like Whole Foods, who at the core had an organic focus, are acquired by tech companies. Amazon itself continues to be rich with resources and gain power through automation and capitalizing on an on-demand culture.

At the same time that companies merge to create even greater forces, people will start to disperse and want more freedom. Remote working is rising in popularity, and that opens up the market for skills to be hired on flexible terms. Gone are the 9-to-5 and the one-company career.

As people disperse and societies become more decentralized because of this new freedom in work, we'll end up with pockets of people who are purpose-driven. Purpose will still unify communities, but can this purpose and can the people have power if everything is too decentralized?

A core manifesto of purpose-driven communities and societies is to stop the ostracization of people and groups. We need to return to our roots as humans and understand that the whole is greater than the parts. Compassion towards oneself and others is essential, and hopefully rising interest in mindfulness will help cultivate that.

In the future, people will still want stuff as fast (if not faster) than they do now. But hopefully, we will see more purpose-driven organizations and people doing good.

In the end, people—not tech, not politics, business or systems—decide what lies ahead in our collective future.

Hopefully these words and predictions will ignite a creative flame for us to continue thinking about and influencing the future for a positive outcome.

Mike Bertolino *is the Global Leader of People Advisory Services for Ernst & Young. Mike leads a global team of over 14,000 practitioners who work with clients every day to help them realize their people agenda—getting the right people, with the right capabilities, in the right place, for the right cost, doing the right things.*

My Dear Ella,

As you take your first steps in the working world, I want to emphasize how the values you've learned and so beautifully embody—empathy, a passion for learning and a global mindset—will guide you in finding your Purpose, and in turn serve as your North Star throughout your professional journey.

I'm still amazed at how digital has transformed every aspect of our lives. To think that your education was nearly completely virtual, yet world-class by any measure, illustrates the power technology has had on redefining entire societal institutions. Every day, you collaborated with students from around the world on nearly every assignment and visited countries and cultures across the planet leveraging cognitive, perceptual, and full-body immersive virtual reality. You leant not only that we are strongest when we team with others, but what it means to celebrate and learn from each other's differences and value the unique perspectives we all possess.

I can recall a time in my career where technology seemed to be on a collision course with the working world. There was a fear that large swaths of the job market would be eliminated, and that people would be left behind as robots and AI encroached upon and ultimately took control of the working world.

But there was a turning point; society realized that for AI to serve humanity brilliantly, for it to unleash its full potential, the algorithms and machine-learning frameworks needed to absorb as many inputs and perspectives as humanly possible. This gave rise to a worldwide shift in thinking—our differences, our diverse backgrounds, our unique experiences, were the secret to developing technology that would take humanity to the next level.

Those fears were quelled when we began to see AI redefine nearly every part of the world; education, finance, even social institutions, our world was transforming faster than we ever thought possible. As a result, the world naturally became more curious about one another, judgement and infighting gave way to curiosity and compassion.

Now, AI is a major part of humanity's toolkit in our quest to solve some of our time's greatest challenges including reversing climate change, creating a universal basic standard of living, eradicating disease, and even exploring what lies beyond our solar system.

It gives me great pride to know how well positioned you are to be a true global citizen, applying your talents wherever you can best serve humanity. You understand the vast possibilities that lie ahead because you have an appreciation for the diversity and scale that this world offers. Through your global education and physical and virtual travels, you've been exposed to more places, people, and points of view than historically possible; elements that will surely aid you in articulating and living your professional purpose.

I am so excited for what lies ahead for you. I encourage you to nurture what I believe are some of your best attributes, your empathy and compassion for others and your global mindset to chart your course in the working world, and beyond.

-Dad

Dearest Enzo,

From my earliest memories of you, I can recall a curious explorer, an adventurer who was continuously amazed with the world around him. You've carried those qualities through into adulthood and as you prepare to define your professional identity, I want to share how excited I am for your future. You're pursuing a life of adventure, professionally and personally, and I couldn't be prouder of you.

Being able to pursue a lifelong career in the gig-economy is something I would have never dreamed possible early in my own professional career.

However, as you're all too keenly aware, technology has the power to transform entire ways of life; the working world is no exception.

The world today reflects the culmination of so many technologies that were nascent only a couple of decades ago. When social media entered the scene, we had no idea how fully integrated it would become into not only our day-to-day lives, but our long-term life planning—shaping opportunities and leading us to explore the world around us through AI-powered recommendations and guidance.

Looking back, there were obvious milestones; when our smartphones began reading facial expressions and cross-referencing that information with location data, machine learning told us which places made us the happiest and recommended places to explore based on how happy we were within various environments.

It wasn't much longer before AI began to tell us what activities made us…happy. Biometric data from wearables was matched with location data and facial recognition to help us understand what we love doing and help us find ways to nurture what makes us happy. I can still recall receiving a notification on my mobile while at our annual holiday charity fundraiser: "Seems like you're enjoying this activity, show similar opportunities?" That was an a-ha moment for me.

It seems natural now that this same machine-learning framework would be applied to the working world and nowhere is this more prevalent than in the gig-economy sector. AI has transformed gig work from a smattering of on-demand roles to a cohesive career path supporting personal purpose, upskilling, reskilling, differential learning, and happiness.

By knowing what activities, assignments, locations, and even people you enjoy the most, gig opportunities will be matched with you. And with so much demand for highly specialized skillsets such as the ones you trained for, there is no shortage of opportunity. The ability to profile the next generation of capabilities needed that are mapped to real-time learning programs will surely keep you ahead of the game and in charge of your career.

You are naturally curious and eager to explore the world. I am truly excited that as a gig worker, you will be able to nurture that curiosity and sense of exploration, traveling to different parts of the world—virtual or physical, supporting top companies and teaming with so many diverse people. I'm further excited knowing that the world has adapted to make this way of life possible for you. From the prevalence of co-living communities, on-demand autonomous transportation, to the advances in cross-border immigration policy, our world is adapting in dynamic ways to support your journey.

I've always tried to impart to you the value of being a lifelong learner. Nowhere is this going to be more important to you than in the gig-economy. Your ability to upskill, spot opportunity, and connect to global educational opportunities will differentiate you and enable you to continually thrive in this space.

I'm so grateful that the natural curiosity and sense of adventure you have always sought out can be further brought to life through a rich, rewarding career in the gig economy. You are a true global citizen and we are so proud of not only where you've been, but where you're headed.

Dad

Michael G. Johnson *is the President and CEO of Johnson Talent Development, a Thought Partner Leadership Coaching firm focused on the development of Next Generation Leaders. He is an Executive Thought Partner, Advisor, Coach, and Speaker around the Future of Talent Management and Leader Development. In 2016, Mike retired as the Chief Human Resources Officer at UPS with over thirty-five years of experience across the entire HR space. Mike combines integrity, big-picture vision, intellect, grit, experience, active listening, and humorous storytelling to connect and inspire others to transform.*

Leadership and Leader Development— What Will It Look Like?

"Lead from the back and let others believe they are in front."
—Nelson Mandela

I think it's a safe bet that leadership and leader development in 2040 will look markedly different than it does today. The larger questions will be what leadership attributes will be most valued, how will leaders be developed, and how will leadership models evolve to meet the demands of work in the new world.

As the generations continue to reshape workforce demographics it will be important for organizations and individuals to also evolve in their leadership style. The quote from Nelson Mandela above is a clarion call to what I believe will be the more prevalent approach to lead in the new world. The days of the command-and-control style of management will end, and a more inclusive, collaborative, curious, and inspirational leadership approach will emerge to replace it. As we continue to look to the future, I believe there will be more emphasis placed on cultivating and identifying leaders who have high emotional intelligence (EQ), a bias toward being inclusionary, high morality, and the ability to guide their teams, allowing the best thinking to emerge. Future leaders will also be charged with creating a wellness environment for their teams where learning, success, and failure without impunity can happen. The next-generation leaders who embrace these necessary and important traits will put themselves and their organizations in the best possible position for success.

One of my favorite stories and quotes came from former United States Secretary of Defense Donald Rumsfeld when asked at a DOD news briefing about the seeming uncertainty of the world post-9/11.

"There are *known knowns*. These are the things we are certain about.... There are *known unknowns*. That is to say, there are the things we know we don't know.... But there are also *unknown unknowns*. These are the things we don't know...we don't know."

I know Secretary Rumsfeld's now-famous "known knowns" quote seems like a riddle or a mental gymnastics puzzle; however, it's a perfect way to analyze the question—what will leadership and leader development look like in twenty years? What are the implications of not evolving leader development within organizations? Who are the key stakeholders?

One of the "known knowns" is that in 2040 the workforce will still be made up of multiple generations. The chart below indicates the approximate ages of the youngest and oldest in each generational cohort in the year 2040:

Generation	Birth Year	Age Range
Gen X	born 1965–1980	60–75
Millennials	born 1981–1996	44–59
Gen Z	born 1997–2015	25–43

Today the average age of CEOs on the Fortune 500 is fifty-seven, with the youngest being thirty-four and the oldest eighty-seven. This means that the CEOs in 2040 could be made up of any of these generations. However, the most likely outcome is we will see the phasing out of the Gen X *manager* and the emergence of the millennial *leader*. I chose the words *manager* and *leader* purposely—for one of the strong traits of the Gen Xer is their ability to manage things, processes, and outcomes, whereas the inherent traits of the millennial will have a bias toward leading people and teams through being better at listening, inspiring, and collaborating with people.

What are the implications for how these new CEOs will lead differently in this world of robots, artificial intelligence (AI), and the on-demand worker, while being influenced by their generational bias?

My best guess is that organizations will see a shift of the average age to younger CEOs primarily due to the speed of dramatic change toward a more interconnected, interdependent, technology-driven, artificial intelligence–led, transparent workplace ecosystem. My prediction is you will see CEOs and certainly senior leadership teams dominated by people from the millennial generation.

Now for some it is shocking, and perhaps scary, to imagine this generation—which has been overhyped stereotypically as aloof, self-absorbed, and fickle—as CEOs. Yet, if you think about how millennials have been socialized, they actually have the perfect set of skills and aptitude to lead their teams through incessant rapid change and long periods of ambiguity that will undoubtedly impact most organizations. Their embedded style of collaboration, fairness, social awareness, and confidence will be needed in leadership more than ever in the history of work.

One question I like to pose to senior leaders when discussing their development processes is, "Picture your leadership pipeline and hone in on the top one or two candidates for your role; now close your eyes and picture them in your job—*tomorrow*. Are they ready?" The typical answer, usually followed by a shocked expression, is "Well, no, they aren't." My follow-up question to them is *why not*, and what are you going to do differently and more intentionally to get them ready?

There are lots of contributing factors to the issue of readiness, one being in the descriptors we use to categorize candidates. What does "ready now" even mean? It certainly lends itself to the visual of the builder constructing a house. First, the foundation is laid, followed by the framing, then electrical, plumbing, drywall, roofing (you get the picture)—and voilà, we have a ready-now house. I believe that in twenty years, if not sooner, careers will be more like the artist creating a work on a blank canvas; it won't be confined by structure, as in career ladders, but will be more fluid, like that of a climbing wall. I believe this career development nomenclature will evolve to better describe candidates' viability or best-fit descriptors to better illustrate a continuum versus a readiness model—fluidity versus building blocks.

Another certainty is the workforce will be more global, more diverse, and more interconnected than at any previous point in history. Today women and people of color make up less than 5 percent of the CEO demographics. In twenty years, that will begin to look dramatically different. What are the leadership development implications for organizations to consider for ensuring they have the right attraction and development model in place? By 2040 I predict that this notion of talking about diversity will end mostly due to the simple fact that workforce demographics will have so significantly shifted that selection of leaders will organically come from a more diverse pool of candidates. The tailwind of the change of leadership teams and CEOs made up of mostly millennials, who aren't constrained by seeing the world through a homogeneous lens, will help stop this endless chase of "fixing" the diversity picture. They have been socialized to see people for who they are and will have a natural lean toward ensuring that teams are ripe with people from all backgrounds, as well as a good gender mix.

Jeff Wald does a great job in this book helping to predict what the future of work will evolve into, but with those predictions comes the uncertainty of the "known unknowns"—what do we know today that will be unknown in 2040, and what implications will these changes have on how leaders will lead in the future?

My belief is conventional leadership models will be challenged in this asymmetrical, black-swan environment, forcing new thinking around how to lead and how to develop future leaders. What is still unknown is just how radically different they will need to be.

As was mentioned in the book, the shift of emphasis to a shareholder capitalism mindset in the 1970s through the 1980s drove organizations to stop looking at employees as assets to be developed, but rather as costs to be maintained. However, by 2040, the continuing shrinkage of working age populations, the labor force participation rate likely still being flat, and new work positions emerging will place more pressure on organizations to rethink how they will maintain a highly engaged core workforce.

Leaders will have to perform in the most difficult of environments. If the Total Talent Management structure that Jeff outlines in the book comes into play, we will be leading the most diverse set of agile teams ever. There will be a mixture of permanent employees, temps, freelancers, robotics, and vendors all working seamlessly on tasks and projects that will be determined and dispatched through an AI engine. The work will be more integrated and the boundaries more permeable, allowing work to flow in and around the constituents that are responsible for making it happen.

There will be an even greater shift to allow work to exist outside the traditional brick-and-mortar walls of offices, so how will leaders keep all their talent motivated, rewarded, and engaged? There will be even more automation of work that is high volume and repeatable. However, as this shift is occurring, there will also be the creation of new work, requiring different capabilities, competencies, and skills. Managing this workplace tension between these two powerful forces will fall at the feet of leaders.

Along with the shift to Total Talent Management processes, there will continue the parallel movement to a Total Personal Responsibility Model, including managing your own development.

One of the glaring gaps in most talent management processes today is identifying talent through a sound set of organizational capabilities and future needs. Most talent processes are too reliant on managers identifying talent and nominating candidates for consideration for more responsibility, and the candidates being placed into a seemingly never-ending maze of career-planning discussions, talent reviews, and selection meetings, where, in most cases, the criteria are obscure or ambiguous. The workplace of 2040 will demand a better mousetrap for development, including transparency, continuous feedback, clarity of job requirements, and more curated development plans for candidates.

I envision that the use of AI engines in talent management processes will have a significant impact on producing more efficient and, I believe, better outcomes for developing leaders. As I mentioned above, most organizations typically have the requisite talent needed within their walls; the challenge for them is having visibility to that talent through a data-rich repository identifying the capacity and capabilities of each individual without the unintended bias of human involvement in identifying, recommending, nominating, and selecting people.

I see, in the future, AI engines providing senior leaders, at the push of a button, with real-time snapshots of their entire workforces with all the relevant data (competencies, capabilities, performance metrics) they need to pinpoint individuals for development who align to organizational needs. From these lists, senior leaders—unencumbered from all the time currently spent on talent reviews, individual career-planning sessions, and organizational needs meetings—now will be able to spend their time on more focused, customized development planning, working with their HR/Talent Management teams to carefully cultivate and curate individual development plans for their talent.

The senior leaders will need to shift their focus from managing talent to creating the right environment for their candidates, where both learning and failure can happen without fatalistic outcomes. The objective will be to provide the candidates the opportunity to exercise their critical thinking muscle while also honing their EQ skills, both of which will be critically needed capabilities in the new world of work.

Equally important to creating the right environment of work assignments and cultivating the needed knowledge, skills, and abilities (KSAs) for future organizational needs will be for the senior leader to be in regular conversation with the candidates. In these structured discussions, the senior leaders will have to be skilled in how to take a coaching stance with their candidates where they can allow them to express their learnings and failings and chart their own course forward. The senior leader will also be listening intently, looking to gauge the candidates' progress and EQ skills development.

This mix of machine and human interaction will be the perfect intersection for a more efficient way to develop future leaders while the senior leader also hones their own development.

With the advent of a new machine learning and influence of work in the future providing organizations with all the key data, what will be missing is the ability to rationalize the data and understand the interdependencies of both the work and the worker. The AI engines will distribute the work, but the leaders of teams will be left to focus on the human experience—how to ensure that people feel connected to the organizational objectives. Leaders will have to be comfortable with working in ambiguity and have strong personal leadership traits. I believe you can distill the most critical personal leadership development skills that will be needed in future leaders to these five traits:

- ► Critical Thinking
  - ○ The soundness of thoughts, data synthesis, judgment, and providing viable solutions
- ► Clear Communications
  - ○ The two most critical lenses
    - ► Clarity of the message
    - ► Active listening
- ► Curiosity
  - ○ Do they have a growth versus fixed mindset—open to new ideas and change?
- ► Credibility
  - ○ The components of trust—reliability, integrity, and influence
- ► Consideration/Cultivation of Others
  - ○ Their emotional intelligence—EQ their self-awareness, awareness of others, and collaboration

As I have outlined here, there will certainly be lots of "knowns," as well as many more *unknowns*, as the world of work evolves in the next twenty years, but one thing is certain—it will be different. The old adage of "the only constant is change" will ring true in the year 2040, adding to it the speed at which it is happening. The implications, I believe we all can agree, will be exacerbated due to the pace of change on multiple dimensions happening simultaneously. I do believe that there are what I like to call the Universal Truths of Leadership—that leadership is hard, yet attainable; people want to be led; inherent in leadership is the need to believe in and connect with people; and it requires vision and communication. I believe that the next generation of leaders will:

- ► Innovate more—using technologies that we can't imagine
- ► Create more—viable winning solutions at a faster pace
- ► Solve more—complex problems

- Collaborate more—with people not like them
- Integrate more—to produce the collective best ideas
- Ask more—not about the "knowns" but the "unknowns"

They will learn better because they will need to, listen better because they want to, and lead differently because they will have to. How the future leaders will tackle the challenges still yet undetermined will be fascinating to watch, but I am confident that they will rise to the challenge.

What are the implications of how you lead through this? Here are some predictions:

- There will be fewer and fewer managers of work. AI will take over most of what is known today as managing the workforce.
- Organizations will have to discover new methods to develop their future leaders. The model of moving talent from position to position to gain the requisite KSAs will change. Leaders will have to learn strategy, innovation, and entrepreneurship principles in different ways.
- Education system will begin offering learning programs that incubate leaders:
    - They have to be an active participant in the development process.
    - That's how universities will show their value and differentiation to students, businesses, and parents.
- People will be given leader attributes, and it will be up to them to manage their own development.
- CEOs will shift their focus more to leading and developing their next generation of leadership.
- The Universal Truths of Leadership will be tested.
- Future leaders will have to be more comfortable working with ambiguity.
- Work and life will be more seamless—the movement from Live-to-Work to Work-to-Live will be complete.

- People will continue to work longer—how will leaders integrate this into their workforce models?
- The typical model used today in leadership development (Pull)—where the organization owns the process of developing and selecting candidates—will shift to more ownership by the individuals (Push).
- Millennials place high value on fairness and equity and will change how people are selected for development and positions—the current development and selection processes are rife with bias both intentional and unintended.
- The length of time to develop leaders will shrink—stretch assignments will give way to learning while leading.
- Ready-now nomenclature (descriptors) will be replaced with Viable for What Positions—today we have these rigid fixed hierarchies; tomorrow the structures will be much more permeable and fluid, so leaders will have to be much more interdisciplinary.
- Career ladders will be replaced by climbing walls—always moving directionally upward but allowing some to step aside and others to step back.

Michelle Greenstreet *is a forward-thinking executive leader and change/transformation agent with an extensive portfolio of success driving human resource and operating strategies and programs across multiple industries in both private and public companies. She has held senior-level positions across several sectors, including financial services, commercial real estate, global manufacturing, and consulting services. She leads with the simple, yet powerful, knowledge that people drive results, and, therefore, she helps organizations create high-impact teams and cultures of inclusion that achieve maximum results.*

The End of Jobs. The Rise of Humanity.

Technology is evolving at an unparalleled pace; the world is shrinking as all the information we need resides in the palm of our hands. Economies continue to ebb and flow, and the war for talent rages on. There is perhaps a more meaningful evolution, or revolution, underway. Perhaps not as noticeable, or newsworthy, and certainly not as swift-moving as flying cars or drones that will deliver our food, our products, and one day our children to and from school and us to and from work (whatever work may be left for us humans to do!).

When asked to contribute to this book, I have been pondering my own "workplace evolution" and the pace of change I have witnessed and sometimes driven in my organization. Thinking about the workplace of 2040 has given me a myriad of visions: some good and some not. I am ill-equipped to speak to the advances of robotics, AI, and the era of digitization. I am excited and fearful of the pace of technological change, the advancement of modern medicine and the impact to life expectancies, climate change, the world economy, and the impact to supply and demand when everyone becomes a fractional worker. As we see glimmers of this today, by 2040 I am confident robots and computers will replace scores of recruiters, doctors, accountants, cooks, truck drivers, and factory workers.

My vision for the workplace of 2040 involves something softer, something quieter, and perhaps less dramatic. My predication of the workplace of tomorrow involves the rise of humanity placed firmly in the center of the employee experience. At present, there is a groundswell of emotion around leadership, culture, and creating "best places to work." Scores of books, podcasts, YouTube videos, and TED Talks are produced annually around helping people become, well, better people. While the focus is presently around building great leaders, defining what a great leader is, and teaching people how to become great leaders, I believe there will be a simple shift in thinking. That shift is about caring. Caring, genuinely caring, about employees. I believe it will be a norm for companies to add caring into the mix of core values. More importantly, I think it will become a staple of existence for a vast majority for organizations, cultures, and leaders. A simple, yet powerful, vision for the notion that caring about your employees becomes commonplace. That idea that being thoughtful, building and having trust between employees, and showing appreciation will be the norm by 2040. It will no longer be a nice-to-have. It will stop being an aspirational notion discussed by (mainly) HR professionals. By 2040 it will be commonplace to care. Authentically and sincerely caring about one another in the workplace.

There is already a movement underway that will fully blossom by 2040 (at least in most advanced nations) that those that care win. By 2040 employees will have demanded and received equality in pay, they will have demanded and received fair treatment, and most importantly they will have demanded and received a workplace where their coworkers and leaders genuinely care about them. Such a simple concept, yet so many miss the mark. There will be a demand, met with ample supply, of authenticity and care in the workplace. Those companies that teach leaders how to care will rise and succeed. Institutions will be teaching leaders and MBA students the impact and relevance of having a heart in business, that is equal to having a brilliant mind. The hundreds of books published annually on leadership can be replaced with one simple dogma—care about your people. You don't have to love them, you don't have to invite them for dinner, but you must care, and you must demonstrate that you care. This will not be the call for more training classes, or more inclusion groups; nor am I predicting we certify a million more executive coaches by 2040.

I am referring to the notion that is unfolding now, and will continue to evolve, that human beings must, and will, care about one another in the workplace. A new world order that leaders begin with caring about all stakeholders and success derives from this place—first. The evolution that is underway now, and will unfold over the next twenty years, is that employees will tolerate nothing less than supervisors, managers, leaders, and executives who care about them. It will be those organizations that celebrate and honor not only the largest intellect but also those that demonstrate they care. Those organizations that care enough to be demanding—demanding of performance, demanding of developing your skills, demanding of creating greatness—will also demand that everyone care and demonstrate this to one another, and to all stakeholders.

Caring won't stop restructurings or poor performance or intimidation or harassment. Caring won't be a cure-all for the jerks and ill-mannered people who will still show up to work. Nor will caring stop companies from failing or cease layoffs and job cuts. But it will ease the pain when these events occur because you will know that those making the decisions did so with a caring and deliberate desire to ease the pain to employees when these decisions were made. By 2040 the rise of humanity in the workplace will have finally risen to a new level—one where fairness is not optional, humanity and heart matter just like a healthy balance sheet, and organizations understand that going from good to great can't happen unless you care.

William Weissman *is a Partner and member of the Board of Directors of Littler Mendelson, P.C., the nation's largest law firm devoted to representing management in labor and employment matters. He leads Littler's Employment Taxes Practice Group and devotes a substantial portion of his practice to worker status issues. He is a frequent speaker and writer on that topic.*

In Elizabethan England, all subjects were required to wear knit caps. The purpose was to artificially create work—jobs—for Queen Elizabeth's subjects. In 1589, William Lee, seeing the time-consuming labor required to produce a knit cap by hand, developed the stocking frame as a way to alleviate some of that hard manual work. When Lee sought a patent from the queen, she rejected the request, observing that the invention would deprive citizens of employment and make them beggars. Recognizing the implications that innovation could have on the status quo, Lee's invention was simply too dangerous to implement. Notwithstanding Queen Elizabeth's astute observation that innovation causes disruption, the stocking frame was put into operation, driving down the price paid for knit caps and changing the nature of work for an entire industry. Tales of the Luddites smashing the stocking frames followed, but such conduct was ineffective: innovation won, protectionism lost.

This same story continues to be played out today. Take ride-sharing apps and their impact upon the livery and taxi industries. Ride-sharing apps are a remarkable innovation that took excess capacity or idle assets and made them productive, while providing opportunities for individuals to earn compensation from using those assets. Ride-sharing apps challenged not merely an industry, but also the way we think about markets. They significantly expanded the marketplace for a service the public wanted—a service that was constrained by government-imposed limitations intended to keep prices artificially high to ensure a reasonable income and stability for livery and taxi drivers. This is just a variation on Queen Elizabeth's protectionism. But by breaking that government-imposed monopoly, ride-sharing apps improved the service the public had access to while providing individuals new work opportunities previously denied them by government controls.

By changing the fundamental economics of the market for transportation services, ride-sharing apps challenged both aspects of the government monopoly—limited services and artificially high prices—and in turn prompted pushback from the industry with the help of government. In 2014, taxi drivers in several European cities staged protests, clogging the streets in major cities, including London, Paris, Berlin, Madrid, and Milan. Protests in the United States were more muted, but in 2015, when New York City Mayor Bill de Blasio sought to regulate ride-sharing apps out of business, the outcry from the public was so strong he had to back down within a week. The tension between ride-sharing apps' innovation and its implications for work in a long-established industry has not finished playing out. The current iteration is just an intermediary step, as self-driving cars likely take over and eliminate the driving aspect of the work, even as new jobs are created both designing and servicing the vehicles.

Our current labor and employment law framework was largely designed to regulate the relationship between individuals and large industrial firms such as US Steel and Standard Oil that arose in the mid-to-late 1800s, or what business historian Alfred Chandler called "center firms." I call this a *firm-centric* legal framework. Some of the fundamental assumptions that underlie our legal framework can be traced back hundreds of years. One is that if individuals are capable of working, they must do so, and the public is not obligated to support them. This concern originates from laws such as the Statute of Laborers in 1351, which forced all able-bodied individuals in Britain to work, which was necessary given the loss of nearly one-third of the population to the Black Plague. Our modern unemployment insurance laws are based on this same assumption: only when an individual is unemployed through "no fault of his own" is he entitled to benefits, and even then only after he worked and earned sufficient wages first.

At the core of our firm-centric legal framework is the erroneous assumption that firms are stable, and thus government can use them to maintain economic stability for individuals. The problem is that firms are remarkably unstable—and getting more so for various reasons.

Polaroid Corporation, once one of the most recognized brands in the world because of its innovations in instant photography, is today nothing but a trade name. Polaroid made several missteps that doomed it, including failing to anticipate and react to the shift to digital photography and engaging in a costly patent war with Kodak. The same creative destruction that propelled Polaroid to the top of its industry for a few decades was the same force that resulted in thousands of employees losing their jobs and retirement savings as the company went through bankruptcy twice in less than a decade.

Forty years ago, the average life expectancy of a Fortune 500 firm was between forty and fifty years, down from about seventy-five years several decades earlier. This lifespan is shorter than that of an individual, but roughly corresponds to the traditional amount of time that a person is in the workforce. Today a firm's lifespan is about eighteen years and shrinking. While the lifespan of firms is shrinking, the length of time an individual spends in the workforce is growing, creating a mismatch between the length of time a person works and the length of time a firm survives. That mismatch has implications for the nature of work from an individual's perspective, because the likelihood of staying with a single firm for one's career is being reduced for no other reason than firms are not lasting as long as careers. This has implications for the structure of our firm-centric legal framework, which initially assumed lifetime employment and thus tethered retirement benefits to longevity.

There are a number of reasons why firms are growing more unstable in our firm-centric framework, including merger-and-acquisition activity, but also how firms are organized and operate. As markets become even more efficient and technology has improved productivity, firms do not need the kind of hierarchical, multidivisional structure that center firms so commonly used. The change in the structure of firms is itself a significant innovation that has implications for work. Telecommuting is a very simple example but has profound implications for the nature of work. As technology makes it possible for individuals to exert control over where and when they work, traditional notions of the relationship between firms and individuals change in ways that our firm-centric legal framework is still trying to address.

Our firm-centric legal framework also assumes that individuals only work for firms to support their economic needs for food, clothing and shelter, and that manual labor is less desirable or bad in comparison to nonmanual labor. These assumptions have always been wrong.

Voltaire observed centuries ago in *Candide*, "Work keeps at bay three great evils: boredom, vice, and need." Confucius advised: "Choose a job you love, and you will never have to work a day in your life." Work, broadly defined, is one of the cornerstones of mankind's existence. Work provides more than food, clothing, and shelter; it feeds our emotional need for self-worth, satisfaction, and meaning in life. These aspects of work are not going to change in twenty years. Articles and books abound about how to find meaning in one's work or doing what you love. Gallup has been polling workers about happiness for over a decade. Nonetheless, our legal framework does not sufficiently take into account that work fulfills individuals' emotional needs in addition to financial needs.

Our legal framework also fails to meaningfully recognize the virtues of manual work, or that nonmanual work has limitations. The US Fair Labor Standards Act (FLSA), enacted in 1938 to provide minimum wages and overtime for working more than forty hours in a week, was largely predicated upon the manual/nonmanual dichotomy, with those performing primarily nonmanual—executive, administrative, or professional—work being exempt from its requirements. In other words, if you think for a living, you can do so for twenty-four hours a day, seven days per week, and our legal framework has no real concern for your well-being.

That mental work is less taxing on the body than physical or manual work is a dubious assumption. In May 2019, the World Health Organization (WHO) classified "burn-out" as a medical diagnosis, defined as "a syndrome" that comes from "chronic workplace stress that has not been successfully managed." Burn-out has "three dimensions: 1) feelings of energy depletion or exhaustion; 2) increased mental distance from one's job, or feelings of negativism or cynicism related to one's job; and 3) reduced professional efficacy." Importantly, the WHO notes that this is an "occupational" issue and should be used "to describe experiences in other areas of life." Burn-out is readily associated with employees who would qualify as exempt under the FLSA.

Based on these and several other assumptions, government sought to create a legal framework intended to smooth out and avoid the business cycles that were devastating from the late 1800s through the Great Depression by taxing the relationship between firms and individuals to fund benefits to offset the negative impacts that occur when the relationship breaks down. This created a self-reinforcing loop that required more employees to pay more taxes to fund more benefits.

In doing so, our legal framework created a system that was inclusive or exclusive based on an either/or status determination: an individual is either an employee entitled to various government protections, or is an independent contractor excluded from them; or, an individual is a nonexempt employee subject to various government protections, or an exempt employee who is not. While there have been changes over time, our firm-centric framework that is designed around segmenting individuals into different groups was perhaps a useful model for large industrial firms, but it is not working well in our modern digital economy.

To create a better legal framework, we need to plan a reasoned, systemic shift from a *firm- centric* legal framework to an *individual-centric* legal framework. An individual-centric legal framework is not one where individuals get to do whatever they want, nor it is one where government merely replaces firms as the vehicle to provide benefits to individuals (such as Medicare for All). Rather, an individual-centric legal framework is one in which government is redesigned to better fit around individuals, instead of fitting individuals into our current model based largely upon artificial statuses that divide us rather than unite us.

Turning back to ride-sharing apps as an example, drivers are treated as independent contractors. Numerous lawsuits over their status assert that they should be employees, and thus firms should provide minimum wages, overtime, and other benefits, which pits individuals who are happy with the model and the flexibility and control against other individuals who are focused on what they perceive to be missed economic opportunities. Government is also interested because of the desire for tax revenue to pay for benefits and ensure economic stability. But should drivers' status as an employee or independent contractor really be a roadblock to innovation? Why must it be all or nothing? The answer of course is because of how our firm-centric legal framework operates.

One problem is tax withholding: employees are subject to it; independent contractors are not. Technology already exists today to solve this problem. When an individual gets into a vehicle for a ride, the payment is electronic. A portion of that payment can be diverted to the government as easily as to the driver, with the financial intermediary also taking its fee, without regard to some artificial status. What is missing today is the infrastructure to make these changes possible. Some haphazard steps have been taken over the years. Independent contractors are subject to self-employment taxes (SECA) that fund Medicare and Social Security, little different from employees who pay taxes to fund those same benefits under what is called FICA. Yet as a society, we expend tremendous amounts of time and expense on distinguishing between employees subject to FICA and independent contractors subject to SECA because of our firm-centric legal framework, despite accomplishing the same purpose regardless of such status.

Another issue is benefits. Contrary to what many probably believe, it is not whether an individual is an employee or independent contractor that is the biggest issue with the provision of health insurance or retirement benefits, but who your employer is in the first place. Employees who work for large, highly profitable firms tend to receive more generous benefits than those who work for small firms or firms with very tight margins. Even in the heyday of large industrial firms in the 1950s, more than half of individuals still worked for small businesses that provided few if any benefits. If society wants to move toward greater equality, decoupling benefits from firms and giving individuals greater control and flexibility over those decisions make sense. The solution is not to create a third category of worker that is partially an employee and partially an independent contractor, as some have proposed, but to make the question of worker status irrelevant in the first place.

Not all innovation must be controversial to have an impact. Take the mundane example of exoskeletons, which are reducing workplace injuries. As the cost of exoskeletons decreases and their use becomes more widely dispersed, disabling workplace injuries will continue to fall. This in turn has serious implications for not only the workers' compensation system, which is a substantial cost to firms, but also the ability of workers to continue in fields such as construction or manufacturing as they grow older. This is taking place in Japan today, which has a shortage of workers and is using innovations such as exoskeletons to keep older workers performing longer. Nonetheless, figuring out how to regulate even relatively noncontroversial technologies such as exoskeletons requires foresight and planning.

Twenty years from now, there will be some small incremental steps toward an individual-centric legal framework, likely greater portability of healthcare benefits, but not nearly enough to fundamentally alter the legal landscape for regulating the relationship between firms and individuals. Too many workers will still be afraid of change and seek government protection, and too much pushback will occur. The battles taking place now will still be playing out.

So I predict that in 2040, a mere five presidential elections from now, work will look a lot like it does today. In twenty years' time we will only be beginning to make the kinds of systemic changes to our firm-centric legal framework that are necessary to provide the kinds of resources that let individuals flourish in the face of rapidly expanding innovations that continue to improve our lives.

ACKNOWLEDGMENTS

IN SPENDING THE LAST FIVE YEARS WRITING THIS BOOK, AND THEN rewriting and then rewriting again, there were countless people who provided thoughts, assistance, and support. Let me start with the men and women who helped me build WorkMarket; if there is no WorkMarket then there is no book. From my co-founder, Jeff Leventhal, to the legendary venture capitalist, Fred Wilson, there are too many people to thank and too many people to whom I am forever grateful. Our founding team, our investors, our advisers, our customers, our partners, and of course the workers on the platform, all played a part in building this great company.

I am thankful to have found the perfect partner to continue WorkMarket's growth in ADP. ADP is blessed with great leaders and operators and I am fortunate to have the chance to work with people like Joe Borelli, Jens Audenaert, Doug Politi, Esra Alev, Jason Ledder, Lorraine Barber Miller, Don Weinstein, and again too many to name, without whom this book would not exist.

As I began to write *The End of Jobs* in 2015 (it was a very different book then) I was helped in the first steps of the journey by Cheryl Strauss Einhorn, Karen Leland, Cari Sommer, and Jonathan Shapiro. They provided that first push out the door on a long and winding journey. Actually, the idea to include contributors was all Cheryl's!

Thank you to the team at Post Hill Press. I may have missed deadline after deadline but you did your best to keep this all on track. Without Anthony I would have never been a published author and I am honored to work with you and your team (especially Maddie and Devon!) again.

Of course, I want to thank the leaders who spent hours writing their sections for Chapter 10, my favorite chapter! They all said "yes" when asked if they would write their vision of the future of work in 2040 and I am so happy with their creativity, their insight and their friendship. I look forward to seeing you all on January 1, 2040 for the awarding of the $10 million Future of Work Prize (and hopefully once or twice before then!).

Lastly, and most importantly, to my family: Without you I would never have found the courage to become the person I am today. The good fortune I had to be born to Phyllis and William Wald, the honor I have to be brothers with Michael and Adam, the joy I feel in having sisters-in-law Julie and Rachel and the pride I can't conceal in seeing the wonderful humans they are raising, Jonah, Eli, Evi, Milo, Iyla, and Ruby; it's all too much for words. Thank you to my amazing and supportive family, I love all you so much.

ABOUT THE AUTHOR

JEFF WALD IS THE FOUNDER OF WORK MARKET, AN ENTERPRISE SOFT- ware platform that enables companies to efficiently and compliantly organize, manage,and pay freelancers (purchased by ADP). Jeff has founded several other technology companies including Spinback (eventually sold to Salesforce). He is an active angel investor and startup advisor, as well as serving on numerous public and private Boards of Directors.

Jeff holds an MBA from Harvard University and an MS and BS from Cornell University. Jeff is the author of *The Birthday Rules* and the upcoming book, *The End of Jobs: The Rise of On-Demand Workers and Agile Corporations*. Jeff was named "One of the 100 Most Influential People in Staffing" by the Staffing Industry Analysts in 2017 and 2018.